WORLD WAR II DAYS

American Kids in History™

WORLD WAR II DAYS

Discover the Past with Exciting Projects, Games, Activities, and Recipes

David C. King

Illustrations by Cheryl Kirk Noll

John Wiley & Sons, Inc.

New York • Chichester • Weinheim • Brisbane • Singapore • Toronto

Copyright © 2000 by David C. King. All rights reserved
Illustrations © 2000 by Cheryl Kirk Noll
Published by John Wiley & Sons, Inc.
Published simultaneously in Canada

Design: Michaelis/Carpelis Design Assoc., Inc.

The publisher and the author have made every reasonable effort to ensure that the experiments and activities in this book are safe when conducted as instructed but assume no responsibility for any damage caused or sustained while performing the experiments or activities in the book. Parents, guardians, and/or teachers should supervise young readers who undertake the experiments and activities in this book.

King, David C.
        World War II days: discover the past with exciting projects, games,
    activities, and recipes / David C. King.
            p. cm.
        Summary: Discusses American life during World War II, depicts a year in the lives of two fictional families, and presents projects and activities, such as deciphering codes, making a mobile out of found objects, and baking a sweet potato pie.
        ISBN 0-471-37101-7
        1. World War, 1939-1945—Miscellanea—Juvenile literature. 2. War games—Juvenile literature. [1. World War, 1939-1945—United States—Miscellanea.] I. Title: World War 2 days. II. Title: World War Two days. III. Title.

    D743.9.K4 2000
    940.53—dc21   00-020474
                                                                    CIP

Printed in the United States of America
10 9 8 7 6 5 4 3 2 1

To all the American kids of World War II days
for serving their country on the home front.

ACKNOWLEDGMENTS

Special thanks to the many people who made this book possible, including: Kate C. Bradford, Diana Madrigal, Diane Aronson, and the editorial staff of the Professional and Trade Division, John Wiley & Sons, Inc.; Susan E. Meyer and the staff of Roundtable Press, Inc.; Marianne Palladino and Irene Carpelis of Michaelis/Carpelis Design; Miriam Sarzin, for her copy editing, Sharon Flitterman-King and Diane Ritch for craft expertise; Cheryl Kirk Noll for the drawings; Steven Tiger, librarian, and the students of the Roe-Jan Elementary School, Hillsdale, New York; and, for research assistance, the staff members of the Great Barrington Public Library, the Atheneum (Pittsfield, Massachusetts), Old Sturbridge Village, and the Farmers Museum, Cooperstown, New York. Historical photographs courtesy of the Still Picture Branch, National Archives; and for historical posters, special thanks to George Theofiles, Miscellaneous Man, New Freedom, PA.

CONTENTS

WORLD WAR II DAYS

INTRODUCTION

World War II, 1941-1945

In the late 1930s, military rulers in Germany and Japan plunged the world into World War II— the most terrifying and destructive war in history. The United States hoped to stay out of the fighting, but that neutrality ended suddenly on December 7, 1941. At dawn on that Sunday, Japanese warplanes launched a devastating attack on the U.S. naval base at Pearl Harbor, Hawaii. Shocked and infuriated by Japan's surprise attack, the American people grimly prepared for war.

America's entry into the war came at a critical time. Nazi Germany and Japan, known as the "Axis" powers, had already conquered much of Europe and eastern Asia. Countries friendly to the United States, called the "Allies," or the "Free World," fought back, but they could not hold out much longer. Only the United States could provide the industrial power and the military might to save England, Russia, and the other Allies.

BUY WAR BONDS

President Franklin D. Roosevelt warned that victory would not come easily, but the American people were ready to do whatever was needed. Many went into military service, until nearly one out of every ten Americans was in uniform; just about everyone in the nation had a friend or family member in service. Every American was affected by the war in other ways as well. For example, peacetime goods almost completely disappeared from the nation's stores because industries had stopped all normal production in order to manufacture war materials. People quickly learned to put up with shortages of everyday items, including gasoline, meat, butter, sugar, shoes, boots, even dish soap and tooth-paste. To make sure that scarce goods were shared fairly, the government issued ration books to everyone; the coupons in each person's book showed how much of each item that person could buy.

Kids, too, were eager participants in the war effort. They took part in air raid drills and learned to do without things like bubble gum, chocolate, metal toys, and new baseballs or footballs. On weekends, they collected scrap metal, old tires, and newspapers to be recycled into war materials. They also made, or collected, clothing for children in war-torn lands, and they bought War Bonds, like Savings Bonds, that helped the government pay the huge war expenses.

With American factories and farms producing enormous supplies of weapons and food, and with several million American soldiers, sailors, and airmen at the fighting fronts, the United States and its Allies soon turned the tide of war. After nearly four years of bitter fighting, the victory was finally won in 1945.

The Donatos and the Andersens

This book follows the Donato family through the spring and summer of 1942, and the Andersen family through the autumn and winter of that year. The Donatos and the Andersens are not real families, but their stories will show what life was like for Americans during World War II.

Eleven-year-old Frank Donato lived in San Francisco, California, with his parents, grandparents, and two sisters—Julie, who was six, and Theresa, who had just turned eighteen. The family had struggled through hard times during the Depression of the 1930s, but now both Frank's parents had good jobs at the naval base on Treasure Island in San Francisco Bay. His mom, Marie Donato, worked as an office clerk, and his dad, Vincent, was a machinist.

For Frank, the war was exciting and sometimes a little scary. He followed the war news every day on the radio and in the newspaper. He was thrilled by the sight of warships heading out to sea under the Golden Gate Bridge while sleek warplanes flew patrols over the coast. And he liked taking part in the scrap drives with his friends, and helping the war effort in other ways. Sometimes, though, when the city's sirens blared the signal for an air raid alert, especially at night, he couldn't help but feel a bit scared as he huddled in the basement with his family waiting for the all-clear.

Twelve-year-old Shirley Andersen and her family lived on a wheat farm in southern Minnesota. The land had been settled by Shirley's great-grandparents after they arrived as immigrants from Sweden in the 1880s, and now the farm was operated by her parents, Helen and John Andersen.

The Andersen family felt the impact of the war within a few weeks of the attack on Pearl Harbor. First, Shirley's brother Karl, who was nineteen, left college to enlist in the army air corps, and then the family's two young farmhands quit to join the army. The farm suddenly seemed deserted and the family wondered how they would manage. They decided that Shirley could take over some of the cooking and housework after school so her mom could help with the farm work. Shirley's little brother, seven-year-old Edmund, would spend afternoons with their Aunt Ramona and her children. Everyone in the family was determined they would produce more crops than ever, even though they were shorthanded.

The Projects and Activities

As you follow Frank Donato, Shirley Andersen, and their families through 1942, you can do many of the things young people did during World War II. Like them, you can invent or decipher secret codes, construct paper airplanes that fly, try recipes from different parts of the country, and make things that could no longer be bought in stores, including toys, games, even a flashlight and a radio that really work. You can complete these projects and activities with materials you have around your home or school, or that can easily be purchased at very little cost. As you have fun with the activities, projects, games, and recipes, you'll feel the past come alive and you'll discover what it was like to be an American kid during World War II days.

CHAPTER ONE

SPRING

In the spring of 1942, Frank Donato and his family were surrounded by signs of the war. Factories and shipyards now operated day and night. At Frank's school, the principal and all the male teachers left to join the army, navy, or coast guard; women would operate the school for the duration of the war.

Day after day, Frank could watch American warships and freighters heading out to sea. At night he watched searchlights fanning the sky, searching for enemy aircraft. Enemy planes could not fly far enough to cross the Atlantic or the Pacific Ocean and bomb American cities, but they could be moved close to the American coast on aircraft carriers. So every time the air raid sirens sounded, people took the alert seriously. Nighttime drills were called "blackouts"; everyone had to be careful that their homes showed no shred of light that might serve as a guide to enemy bombers.

HELPING ON THE HOMEFRONT

Frank was eager to do his part for the war effort and he soon learned that there were many ways for kids to help. He went on scrap drives with his friends almost every week, collecting newspapers, old tires, and all sorts of junk made of metal. At school, he began using part of his allowance to buy War Stamps, working toward saving enough for his first War Bond. At home, he was in charge of tying newspapers in bundles, cleaning and flattening tin cans, saving cans of cooking fat, and peeling the tinfoil off candy and gum wrappers.

Frank also looked for ways to make things that were no longer available in stores. His father helped him with his first project—making a little flashlight to use during blackouts. When the government asked people to plant "victory gardens," he persuaded the whole family to join in. By growing some of their own table vegetables, families like the Donatos would enable

farmers to raise more food for the armed forces and for the nation's allies.

Nonna (grandma) Donato, who had grown up on a farm in Italy, gave directions to Frank and his sisters, Julie and Theresa, on how to begin their garden. They dug up the Donatos' back lawn, then the front, replacing the grass with neat rows of lettuce, beans, tomatoes, and other crops. As soon as they could pick the first leaves of lettuce, Frank and Nonna made their first "victory salad."

PROJECT VICTORY SALAD

When the government first urged people to plant victory gardens in January 1942, millions of Americans responded. The gardeners soon found that they were not only helping the war effort, they were also getting some exercise, eating healthier meals, and enjoying the time spent with family members and neighbors.

Newspapers and magazines helped by providing a steady stream of new recipes and serving suggestions, especially for the standard tossed salad. Gardeners discovered that adding a few slices of ham or bacon to a salad provided a good way to stretch their limited meat supplies. A salad with slices of meat had traditionally been called a "chef's salad," but Americans in 1942 preferred the more patriotic name of "victory salad."

In planning your victory salad, you don't have to use all of the ingredients listed, but try for six or seven, including meat. You'll also find that your victory salad provides a good way to use leftover cooked vegetables, like peas or green beans.

INGREDIENTS

small head of Boston or iceberg lettuce
6 to 8 leaves romaine lettuce or endive
2 small tomatoes
4 to 6 radishes
3 or 4 scallions (or substitute 1 slice red onion)
2 hard-cooked eggs
6–8 ripe olives (pitted)
2 or 3 canned artichoke hearts
4 to 6 uncooked mushrooms
½ to 1 cup cooked ham, salami, chicken, or turkey meat—or some of each
1 teaspoon lemon juice
1 avocado
leftover cooked vegetables (optional)
3 to 4 tablespoons grated Parmesan or Romano cheese
dash salt and pepper
bottled salad dressing

EQUIPMENT

colander or large kitchen strainer
paper towels
large salad bowl
cutting board
paring knife
vegetable chopper (optional)
small bowl
salad spoon and fork (or two forks)
cruet or small pitcher for salad dressing
adult helper

MAKES

about 6 servings

Gardening for the War Effort

Americans were very proud of their victory gardens, and they planted them wherever there was enough soil, sunlight, and water. At schools throughout the country, students planted large gardens to supply the school cafeteria. Factory workers did the same. In many suburbs and small towns, the volunteer fire companies plowed large fields, assigned plots to every family that signed up, and used fire hoses to keep crops moist when rainfall failed. City dwellers planted gardens on rooftops, in vacant lots, and in window boxes.

Critics of the program predicted that the gardeners would lose interest when the novelty wore off. That didn't happen. In 1943, Americans planted almost 21 million victory gardens. And in 1944, the last full year of the war, victory gardens supplied more than 40 percent of the nation's fresh vegetables.

1. Place the lettuce in the colander or strainer and wash it under cold running water. Let the running water help separate the leaves of the head of lettuce.

2. Break off bite-size pieces of lettuce with your fingers. Discard any wilted pieces.

3. Pat the lettuce dry with paper towels and place it in the salad bowl. Cover the bowl with a damp paper towel and put it in the refrigerator.

4. Wash the other vegetables under cold running water and pat them dry on paper towels.

5. With an adult's help, use a cutting board and paring knife (or a vegetable chopper) to cut the tomatoes, radishes, scallions, ripe olives, eggs, artichoke hearts, and mushrooms into small pieces—about half of bite-size.

6. Cut the ham, salami, chicken, or turkey meat into strips about 1 inch long.

7. Pour the lemon juice into a small bowl and add about ½ cup of water. Have your adult helper peel the avocado, cut it into small pieces, and dip the pieces in the lemon water. This will keep the avocado from turning dark.

8. Remove the salad bowl from the refrigerator and discard the paper towel. With a salad fork and spoon, or two forks, mix in the chopped vegetables, egg, meat, and avocado. You can also add leftover cooked vegetables if you have them.

9. When you're ready to serve, sprinkle the grated cheese, salt, and pepper over the salad. Pour on a small amount of dressing and toss the salad with the fork and spoon, or two forks. Serve extra dressing in a small pitcher or cruet.

 **VICTORY GARDEN**

Gardening, even on a small scale, is fun and rewarding, and there's a special thrill to enjoying your first harvest. If you don't have outdoor garden space available, you can still achieve excellent results with window boxes or flower pots. In fact, even if you have an outdoor garden, it's a good idea to start your seeds in containers indoors to give you better control over growing conditions.

The keys to gardening success are simple: good soil, warmth, plenty of sunshine, adequate water, and enough space between plants. The best guide for each type of plant is the set of instructions on the seed packet. Don't try to do too much, especially working with indoor containers. Leaf lettuce, radishes, scallions, and carrots make good starter vegetables. Above all, be patient. Your seeds will take a week or more to sprout, so don't lose heart when green shoots fail to appear overnight.

MATERIALS

paper and pencil

1 seed packet each for leaf lettuce, radishes, carrots, scallions

2 or 3 window boxes, at least 20 inches long and 6 to 8 inches deep, or 4 or 5 large flower pots, 10 to 12 inches in diameter

pail of coarse gravel or pebbles for drainage
garden topsoil, enough to fill all the containers
peat moss, potting soil, or all-purpose fertilizer
   (optional)
gardening trowel or an old kitchen mixing spoon
4 or 5 craft sticks or popsicle sticks
permanent marking pen, any color
hoe or rake for outdoor plots

1. Plan your garden or containers on paper. Read the directions on the seed packets to get an idea of the space needed between plants and the depth of the soil, then make a sketch of where you will plant each kind of seed.

2. For window boxes and flower pots, fill the bottom of the container with a 1 to 2 inch layer of gravel or pebbles for drainage. Add topsoil to within 1 inch of the top. If the soil feels hard and does not break up easily, use a trowel to stir 1 to 2 cups of peat moss or potting soil into the soil in each container. A small amount of all-purpose fertilizer can also help; follow the instructions on the bag.

3. Use the tip of the trowel or a craft stick to make a shallow groove or furrow in the soil for planting the seeds for each kind of plant. Check seed packets for directions on how deep and how far apart to plant the seeds.

4. Cover the seeds with soil. Lightly press the soil down with the heel of your hand or the trowel.

5. Use the marking pen to write the name of each type of seed on a craft stick. Press the sticks into the soil to mark the location of each variety.

6. For outdoor gardening, loosen the soil with a hoe or rake. The directions on the seed packets will tell you when to transplant from containers to the ground.

7. Your garden won't need a great deal of attention. If possible, place your containers outside for sunlight and moisture. Water the plants as needed, but avoid letting them become waterlogged. Thin the seedlings (pull some out to make more room for the others) when necessary, according to the directions on the seed packets.

8. Your first harvests are likely to be radishes and leaf lettuce—about 1 month after planting (see the chart on this page for harvest times of other vegetables). The only way to tell when root plants like radishes and carrots are ready is to pull one up (although experienced gardeners can often tell by poking a finger into the soil next to the plant). When leaf lettuce forms, pinch off the leaves with your fingers and more leaves will form, giving you several lettuce harvests.

Gardening Tips

1. Unless you have a large outdoor plot, avoid vine plants, such as cucumber, squash, and melons because they spread in all directions.

2. Tomatoes are difficult to grow from seeds, but you can buy seedlings already started. Two or three tomato plants can do well in flower pots, especially the smaller varieties.

3. Good soil is usually dark in color and crumbles easily.

4. If some seeds don't sprout, it's usually because they were planted too deep or the soil was packed too tightly.

5. Plants will usually give you early signs of trouble; they droop when they need water, or form brown spots when they've had too much.

6. Number of days from planting to harvest:

leaf lettuce	**bell peppers**
35–45 days	65–75 days
carrots	**corn**
65–70 days	75–85 days
scallions	**tomatoes**
55–60 days	50–80 days,
radishes	depending
30–35 days	on variety

V for Victory

V for Victory was one of the most important patriotic symbols of World War II. The idea was started by a Belgian who escaped to England when German troops occupied his homeland in 1940. From England, he made radio broadcasts to Belgium and, during each broadcast, he urged people to write the V wherever they could to show their defiance of Hitler's Nazi Germany. The Belgian refugee ended each broadcast with the Morse Code V: dot, dot, dot, dash.

The letter V soon appeared all over Europe, scrawled on walls and pavement. People signaled the Morse Code V by honking car horns, whistling, or knocking on doors. In some languages, the letter had a different, but important meaning. In Dutch, for instance, V stood for Vrÿheid (VREE-hide), meaning "freedom," and in Serbian for Viteštvo (VEETS-vo), the word for "heroism." Americans, too, quickly picked up the idea and, like Europeans, often flashed the V with their index and middle fingers. Throughout the war, newspapers and magazines printed the word Victory with a capital V.

PROJECT HOMEMADE FLASHLIGHT

Throughout the war, Americans found creative ways to deal with the many shortages. Some owners of delivery trucks, for example, who could no longer find tires, made their own out of blocks of wood. And, when nylon stockings were no longer available because nylon was used for making parachutes, many women solved the problem by using tan makeup on their legs and drawing a dark line down the backs of their legs to look like stocking seams.

In this activity, you'll make a homemade flashlight, following the same directions kids used in the 1940s when flashlights were no longer available in stores. These flashlights did not send a very good direct beam, but kids found they worked just fine for reading under the covers at night or during blackouts. And, like kids in World War II days, you can also use your flashlight to send the dot-dash messages of Morse code. With a friend, use the Morse Code chart to exchange brief messages across short distances. A popular message during the war was dot, dot, dot, dash—V for Victory.

Note: This activity is perfectly safe. You won't be using household electrical current and there is no danger of even the mildest electrical shock.

MATERIALS
6-inch piece of single-strand doorbell wire, available in hardware stores or departments
penknife
pliers (narrow, needle-nose pliers, if available)
transparent tape
1 D flashlight battery
1 standard flashlight bulb
adult helper

1. Have an adult help you use the penknife to scrape about 1 inch of insulation off each end of the wire.

2. Use the pliers to bend one end of the wire into a tight, springlike coil, like the coil you see inside many flashlights. Tape the coil firmly to the bottom of the battery, as shown. Make sure that part of the wire presses against the small circle on the base of the battery; this circle is the battery's negative terminal.

3. Wind the other end of the wire tightly around the base of the flashlight bulb, fitting it into the grooves of the bulb. The wire should fit snugly, so you don't have to tape it in place. (Add a little tape, if necessary, but don't cover the very bottom of the bulb.)

4. Tape the middle part of the wire to the side of the battery. Leave enough untaped wire at the top so that you can bend the wire down and press the base of the bulb against the positive terminal of the battery, as shown in the drawing.

5. Your flashlight is now ready. To operate, simply press down on the wire, as shown, until the base of the bulb touches the positive terminal.

You'll quickly see how easy it is to turn the flashlight on and off, and how to use it to flash signals. If at any time your flashlight doesn't work, make sure that the wire is in contact with both the positive and negative terminals.

Morse Code Chart

A dot would be represented by a short flash of your light, a dash by a slightly longer flash. To indicate the end of one letter and the beginning of the next, flash for 5 seconds between letters. Flash for 7 seconds between words.

A · —	M — —	Y — · — —
B — · · ·	N — ·	Z — — · ·
C — · — ·	O — — —	1 · — — — —
D — · ·	P · — — ·	2 · · — — —
E ·	Q — — · —	3 · · · — —
F · · — ·	R · — ·	4 · · · · —
G — — ·	S · · ·	5 · · · · ·
H · · · ·	T —	6 — · · · ·
I · ·	U · · —	7 — — · · ·
J · — — —	V · · · —	8 — — — · ·
K — · —	W · — —	9 — — — — ·
L · — · ·	X — · · —	0 — — — — —

CIVILIAN WARRIORS

Both of Frank's grandparents became civilian defense volunteers. Grandpa Donato, who had migrated from Italy in the 1890s, was very proud when he was selected to be an air raid warden. With his official white helmet, armband, and whistle, he helped patrol their neighborhood during blackouts to make sure that no lights were visible.

Nonna Donato was assigned to the Ground Observation Corps as an aircraft spotter. In March, she joined a team of spotters to set up an observation post on a lonely stretch of beach south of the city. The spotters reported every airplane they saw to the Army Filter Center as part of the nation's warning system to guard against a surprise enemy air attack.

Frank would sometimes join his grandmother at her post on Saturdays. While the spotters chatted and surveyed the skies from an old fishing shack, he collected driftwood, shells, and other objects from the rocky shore. One of the spotters, a man named Wilson, showed

Frank how to assemble some of his finds into a carefully balanced mobile. Mr. Wilson also showed him how to estimate the altitude of aircraft by the form of any nearby clouds. Together they made a chart of the ten major cloud types and the altitudes at which they are normally found.

PROJECT 3-D CLOUD CHART

In 1803, a British pharmacist named Luke Howard devised a system for classifying clouds into three main forms, or types: *cirrus* clouds, from the Latin word for a "lock" or "wisp" of hair; *cumulus,* meaning a "pile" or "heap"; and *stratus,* from the Latin for "layered" or "spread out." Later, scientists added *alto,* meaning "high," and *nimbus,* Latin for "dark rain cloud," to create a classification system of ten major cloud formations that is still in use today.

Early in World War II, Army officials thought aircraft spotters could help identify the altitude of aircraft by referring to whatever clouds they saw. The system didn't work very well for spotting aircraft, but Army Air Force officials found that the additional information did help them predict approaching weather conditions.

In this project, you'll use cotton and paint to make a three-dimensional chart of the ten basic cloud forms. The chart will make an attractive wall hanging for your room, and you can also use it to make a daily check on the cloud and weather conditions where you live.

MATERIALS

several sheets of newspaper
white or light blue poster board, about 12-by-16-inches
poster paint, blue, white, black
paintbrush, about 1-inch wide
ruler
pencil
felt-tip pen, black, medium point
cotton, about half of a 4-ounce box
white glue
paper cup or small dish for mixing paint
small paintbrush
transparent tape
10- to 12-inch piece of string

1. Spread several sheets of newspaper over your work surface and place the poster board on top.

2. If the poster board is white, apply one coat of blue poster paint, using the 1-inch brush. Thin the paint with a little water, if necessary, to create a skylike blue. Allow the paint to dry for 10 to 15 minutes. Apply a second coat, if needed.

3. Use the ruler and pencil to divide the poster board into 3 main sections for high, middle, and low clouds. Darken the lines with the felt-tip pen. Print the labels for the three sections and for the ten cloud types, as shown in the drawing.

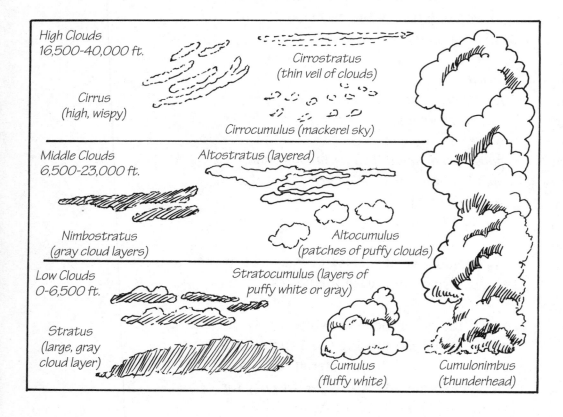

High Clouds
16,500-40,000 ft.

Cirrus
(high, wispy)

Cirrostratus
(thin veil of clouds)

Cirrocumulus (mackerel sky)

Middle Clouds
6,500-23,000 ft.

Altostratus (layered)

Nimbostratus
(gray cloud layers)

Altocumulus
(patches of puffy clouds)

Low Clouds
0-6,500 ft.

Stratocumulus (layers of
puffy white or gray)

Stratus
(large, gray
cloud layer)

Cumulus
(fluffy white)

Cumulonimbus
(thunderhead)

4. To apply your cotton clouds, start at the top of the chart and work your way down. For cirrus clouds, break off small pieces of cotton and stretch the pieces out to create the wispy look of this cloud type, commonly known as "mare's tails." Put a thin strip of glue on the chart where you want to place each wisp and gently press it in place.

Tip: Handle the cotton as little as possible to prevent the clouds from flattening out.

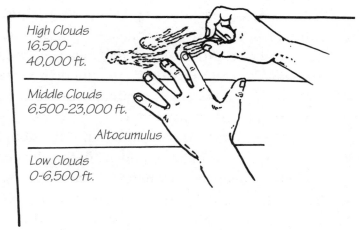

High Clouds
16,500-
40,000 ft.

Middle Clouds
6,500-23,000 ft.

Altocumulus

Low Clouds
0-6,500 ft.

5. Follow the same procedure for the other four all-white clouds—cirrocumulus, cirrostratus, altocumulus, and altostratus—shaping the cotton to look as much like the picture of each cloud as possible.

6. The five cloud types that are lowest in the sky include dark rain clouds and also some forms that may be a mixture of gray and white. You can create various shades of gray for these clouds by mixing black and white paint in a paper cup or small dish. Notice that some cloud formations (cumulus, cumulonimbus) often are gray at the bottom and very white at the top. Others, like nimbostratus and stratus, are solid gray. Use a small paintbrush to make each of your cloud forms as realistic as possible. Paint the cloud pieces and let the paint dry before you glue them to the chart. Then, after gluing a cloud to the chart, add touch-ups of paint wherever needed.

7. To hang the chart, tape a piece of string across the back, about 3 inches from the top. Use 2 pieces of tape in an X shape on each end of the string, as shown, and hang the chart from a pushpin or thumbtack.

Your 3-D cloud chart is now ready to display and use.

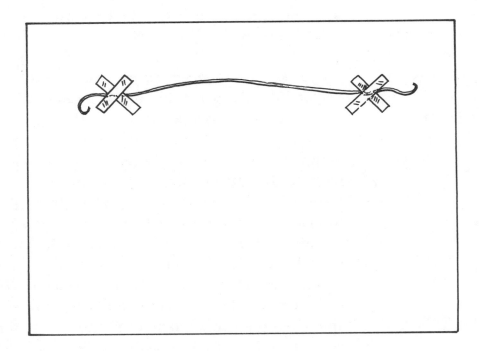

The Danger of Air Attack

The volunteers of the Ground Observation Corps operated their posts day and night throughout the war. More than 600,000 women and men served as spotters in those lonely stations.

Except for three minor incidents, neither Germany nor Japan ever launched a serious threat to the American mainland. In one incident, a Japanese submarine surfaced off the California coast in February 1942, and fired twenty cannon shells at an oil refinery, inflicting little damage. Six months later, a lone Japanese seaplane, transported across the Pacific in a submarine, dropped fire bombs on forests in Oregon, but the fires were easily put out. In the third incident, late in the war, Japan launched thousands of high-altitude balloons equipped with bombs designed to drift on air currents across the Pacific. About 300 of the balloon bombs did reach the United States and Canada, causing several deaths and a few fires. The U.S. government did not release news of the bombs, so the Japanese assumed the scheme was a complete failure and ended it.

PROJECT FOUND-OBJECT MOBILE

In the 1930s, a famous American artist and sculptor named Alexander Calder created a new art form that became known as the *mobile*. Calder had been fascinated by the way circus acrobats kept their balance even when they were moving. He wanted to make sculptures that would show that same combination of balance and movement. After he built a large mobile for the New York World's Fair in 1939–1940, the popularity of mobiles spread and people began making mobiles as a form of home decoration.

You can make your mobile out of any collection of small objects, such as toys or parts of old toys, small tools, objects cut out of paper or cardboard, or things you pick up on a hike or at a beach. Look for interesting shapes and colors to add to your collection—stones, twigs, shells, feathers, pinecones, bits of bark, and a few larger twigs or branches to use as cross pieces.

MATERIALS
several sheets of newspaper
4 or 5 branches or large twigs, 6 to 14 inches long
strong black thread or fishing line
scissors
collection of shells, bark, pinecones, twigs, or other small objects
cup hook
adult helper

1. Spread several sheets of newspaper on your work surface. Place your collection of found objects on top.

2. Choose one large twig or branch for your main cross piece. Tie a piece of thread or fishing line at about the middle and tie it to a temporary location where it will be easy to reach while you're working on the mobile.

3. The key to a mobile is balance. You can add two or more pieces at a time and you can add more cross pieces as long as the mobile is balanced when you're finished. All of the cross pieces should be horizontal and all pieces should move freely without bumping into other elements of the mobile. The only way to achieve this balance is to experiment. Every time you add a new cross piece, or a new object, you will upset the balance. Figure out what you can add or move to restore the balance. Don't be afraid to make mistakes. Instead, have fun moving pieces around, changing the length of the line or the position of the objects on a cross piece.

4. Tie each object tightly to a cross piece, using a short piece of thread or fishing line.

5. When your mobile is complete, ask your adult helper to assist you in hanging it using the cup hook. Hang the mobile in a place where it can turn freely, from the ceiling if possible. The air currents in your room will slowly turn the pieces, creating a constantly changing work of art.

WARTIME EVENINGS

Every evening after dinner, the Donato family gathered in the living room to listen to the radio news. Throughout the early months of 1942, the news was usually bad, as the military forces of Germany and Japan continued their conquests. Then, one evening in early June, the Donatos were thrilled to hear that the U.S. Navy had won a major victory over a Japanese fleet at the Battle of Midway, west of Hawaii. For the first time in the six months following Pearl Harbor, the advance of the Axis powers had been stopped.

Following the news, the Donatos often listened to one or two favorite shows, like *Jack Benny* or *The FBI in Peace and War*. Then, as Julie headed up to bed and Grandma and Grandpa went for a stroll or sat on the porch, Frank's dad went back to his newspaper and his mom finished her evening clothes mending, reading, or letter writing. Frank usually spent an hour with Theresa, playing a favorite game or making a new one. They had fun with a puzzle of colored blocks they made with instructions from a how-to magazine, and the same magazine showed them how to make a board game called Ludo.

Now and then their evening routines were turned topsy-turvy by the air-raid sirens. When the sirens sounded, they rushed to turn off the lights and get to the basement, while Grandpa Donato went out to patrol the streets as an air raid warden.

PROJECT · THE GAME OF LUDO

The ancient game of pachisi, from India, became popular in Europe and America in the 1700s. A simpler version of the game, called Ludo, was developed in the late 1800s and became one of the many popular board games Americans played during the war years.

While Ludo involves a good deal of luck in the roll of the die, there is also room for strategy. Each player has four game pieces to move around the board, and has to decide which piece to move on each roll of the die. Should he or she try to move a piece closer to home? Or try to capture an opponent's piece, forcing that piece to go back to home and start over? The strategy becomes even trickier if three or four people are playing, because there are more opposing game pieces to work around.

MATERIALS

white or light gray poster board, 18 inches square
ruler
pencil
red, blue, yellow, and green crayons or colored pencils
scraps of poster board or cardboard for game pieces
drawing compass or round object, such as a quarter
scissors
one die
2, 3, or 4 players

1. Place the poster board on your work surface. With ruler and pencil, draw parallel lines at 6-inch intervals to divide the board into nine 6-inch squares. Connect the corners of the center square to form an X.

2. As shown in this picture, make 3 columns of game spaces. Each game space is 2 inches wide and 1 inch high. The best way to keep the lines even and parallel is first to make pencil marks along the sides at 1-inch intervals, then join the marks.

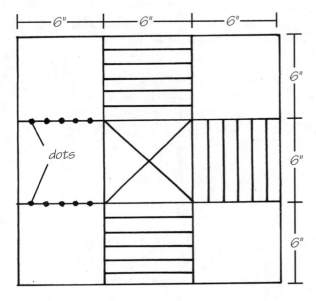

dots

3. With colored pencils or crayons, shade in the home areas for each of the four players—red, blue, yellow, and green—as shown in the next illustration. Be sure to shade in the last 5 spaces in the central section leading to the home goal. Once a player has a game piece in any of those 5 spaces, that piece cannot be captured.

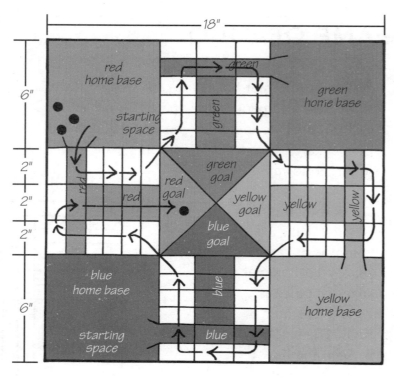

4. Use scraps of poster board or cardboard to make 4 game pieces in each color—red, blue, yellow, and green. Using a drawing compass, a quarter, or a similar round object as a guide, outline 16 pieces, cut them out with scissors, and color them on both sides. You're now ready to play Ludo. The goal is to be the first to move all four of your game pieces around the board and into the home goal.

5. Rules for Ludo

(a) Each player chooses a color for his or her home area and game pieces, then makes one roll of the die. The highest number goes first and the other players follow in a clockwise pattern.

(b) Each game begins with no game pieces on the board. In order to place a game piece on the starting space, a player must roll a 6. If a 6 is not thrown, it's the next player's turn.

(c) A player who throws a 6 is allowed to move a game piece, and then roll a second time. Players **cannot** divide a number rolled between two game pieces, moving one piece 4 spaces, for example, and another 2 spaces on a roll of 6. But, after rolling a 6 and moving a game piece, the player can use the second number thrown to move any of his or her 4 game pieces. This rule can be useful for capturing an opponent's game piece.

(d) Players move their game pieces around the board in a clockwise direction, as shown, using the middle column of spaces only for approaching the player's home goal.

(e) Once a player is in the middle column, a game piece can be moved into the home goal only by rolling the die the exact number of spaces needed.

(f) When a player's game piece lands on a square occupied by an opponent, the opponent's game piece is captured and sent back to its home base to start over. When a game piece has entered the last 5 spaces leading to its home goal, however, it cannot be captured.

(g) The game is over when one player has moved all 4 of his or her pieces into the home goal.

PROJECT COLORED-CUBE PUZZLE

Americans in the 1940s were fond of all sorts of puzzles, including the crossword puzzles in the daily newspaper, puzzle rings, hidden pictures, and objects that could only be fitted together in a brain-teasing way. In this activity, you'll make a puzzle that has been popular since the 1890s. The object of the puzzle is to place the four colored cubes, or blocks, in a row so that each side of the row shows each of the four colors: red, yellow, blue, and white. (The end faces don't count as part of the row.)

You can use any four blocks or cubes of the same size. Children's alphabet blocks are perfect, or you can often find unpainted blocks in hobby or craft stores. You can even use objects as small as dice. If you want to save the cubes for other uses, you can tape the color squares on rather than gluing them.

MATERIALS

several sheets of newspaper
4 blocks or cubes, all the same size
1 or 2 sheets of white paper
pencil
ruler
red, blue, and yellow crayons, colored pencils, or
*   marking pens*

scissors
white glue or transparent tape

1. Spread several sheets of newspaper on your work surface.

2. Place one of the blocks on a sheet of white paper. Trace around it with pencil, making a square the same size as one face of the block.

3. Use a ruler, or one of the blocks, to draw five more squares in a T shape, as shown in the illustration. Notice that, if you fold on the lines, the squares will cover all six sides, or faces, of a block.

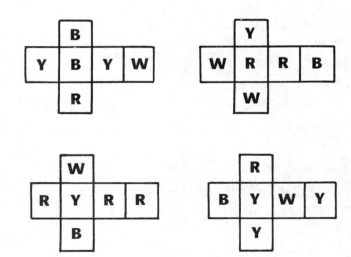

Dangers at Sea

During the early months of 1942, German submarines, called U-boats, roamed the Atlantic Ocean preying on Allied cargo ships. Between January and May, a shocking total of 360 American and Allied ships were sunk by the dreaded U-boats. People living along the Atlantic Coast actually helped the Germans without meaning to. Lights from homes, businesses, and automobiles made the freighters and oil tankers stand out in silhouette, making them easy to see from the submarines farther out at sea. In March 1942 alone, thirty-five ships burned and sank within sight of the American coast.

Towns and states along the coast soon developed the practice of "dim-outs" every night, so that lights on shore did not make the ships stand out. The American, Canadian, and English navies also reduced the U-boat menace by making convoys of ships. Instead of a single merchant ship crossing the Atlantic to carry supplies to England or Russia, a dozen or more ships would form a group, with several warships to protect them from attack.

4. Repeat step 3 to draw three more sets of squares, one for each block or cube.

5. Use crayons, colored pencils, or marking pens to color the T-shaped strips. Carefully follow the color pattern shown; white squares, of course, don't have to be colored. Block 1 will have 2 blue faces, 2 yellow, 1 red, and 1 white. When you fold the strip on the lines, the white face will be on the bottom. Notice that each of the blocks will have a different color pattern.

6. After all of the strips have been colored, cut each T-shaped strip out with scissors. Fold on the lines in order to wrap each strip around a block. Glue each square to a block face, or fix it in place with transparent tape.

7. Your puzzle is now ready. See how quickly you can arrange the blocks so that each row of faces shows all four colors, as illustrated.

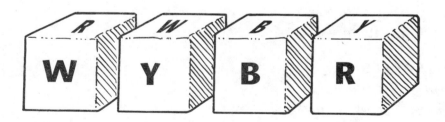

CHAPTER TWO

SUMMER

Late in June, Frank's sister Theresa told the family that she wanted to join the women's branch of the army. This unit, which became known as the Women's Army Corps, or WACs, was just being formed, and Theresa hoped to be one of the first recruits. The WACs would take over jobs that would allow more men to go to the fighting fronts. The whole family proudly accompanied Theresa to the train station when she left for basic training at an army camp in Iowa.

Even before Theresa left, the Donatos had a plan for her empty bedroom. They wrote to Frank's Aunt Florence in Brooklyn, inviting her and her daughter Sophie to come live with them until the war was over. Florence's husband, Dominic Donato, was a navy seaman, serving with the Pacific Fleet; by moving to San Francisco, Florence would have a better chance of seeing him when he had shore leave on the Pacific coast.

PROJECTS

THE GAME OF
SEA BATTLE

PAPER AIRPLANE

JET-POWERED
FLIGHT TEST

PERISCOPE

CONEY ISLANDS

PHILADELPHIA
SOFT PRETZELS

CRYSTAL RADIO

SOUND EFFECTS

COUSIN FROM BROOKLYN

Frank scarcely remembered his cousin Sophie, who was nearly a year older than he. Her family had left San Francisco for Brooklyn almost six years earlier, and the two families had not been together since. Neither Sophie's dad nor Frank's parents were ever able to take enough time from work for the long cross-country train trip, and airplane flights were too expensive.

After a tearful family reunion at the train station, Aunt Florence and Sophie settled into the Donatos' snug bungalow. Six-year-old Julie was delighted to share her room with her cousin, and Frank was pleasantly surprised at how well he and Sophie got along. She enjoyed working in the victory garden, and she helped him with his chores, even taking over the task of cleaning and flattening tin cans. And, because her dad was serving with the Pacific Fleet, she knew a lot about the naval battles in the Pacific.

Sophie also shared Frank's interest in making things. They worked together to construct a toy periscope, imitating the periscopes used on submarines. They had contests with the paper airplanes they made, and Frank demonstrated the principle of jet-powered flight. Sophie taught him several new games, including one called Sea Battle that became his favorite.

PROJECT — THE GAME OF SEA BATTLE

The naval Battle of Midway in June 1942, combined with the Battle of Coral Sea a month earlier, marked a turning point in the Allies' war against Japan. After Midway, the Japanese made no more advances; instead, they began a slow and steady retreat that ended with their final surrender more than three years later.

Coral Sea and Midway were historic in another way. These battles were the first in history in which the opposing ships never came within sight of each other. The battle was fought almost entirely by the warplanes launched from American and Japanese aircraft carriers. The game of Sea Battle is not unlike the battles at Midway and the Coral Sea as each player attempts to "sink" an enemy fleet without knowing where any of the "ships" are located.

MATERIALS

4 sheets of plain paper or graph paper
ruler
2 pencils
copy machine, if available
2 players

1. On plain paper or graph paper, use a ruler and pencil to make a grid of 144 squares, 12 squares across and 12 down. If you're using plain paper,

begin by drawing a 6-inch square. Mark dots every ½ inch on all four sides of the square, then connect the dots to produce a perfect grid.

2. Write the letters A to L down the side of the grid, as shown, and the numbers 1 to 12 across the top.

3. Copy the grid on separate sheets so that each player has two copies. If you have access to a copy machine, you can run off multiple copies for future games.

4. For each player, label one sheet the Defense Grid and the other sheet the Attack Grid.

5. Each player has five ships, which are placed anywhere on the Defense Grid, making sure that the opponent doesn't see these locations. The drawing shows an example of ship placement. The five ships are: two aircraft carriers (shade in 4 squares for each); one battleship (3 squares); and two

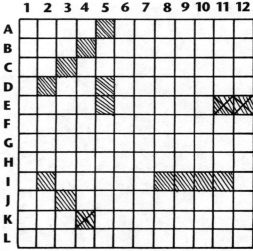

Defense Grid

Kids' Contributions

While American kids played all sorts of games in the early 1940s, they also used their spare time to make important contributions to the war effort. One way they helped was by buying War Stamps and Bonds at school to help pay the enormous costs of the war. In 1944 alone, school sales of War Bonds provided enough money to pay for 2,900 airplanes, 44,000 jeeps, and 11,700 parachutes.

Kids were also the most ambitious collectors of scrap materials. In June 1942, for example, President Roosevelt announced that the nation needed scrap rubber. Within weeks, the Boy Scouts had collected 54,000 tons, mostly in old tires. In addition, the need for workers led most states to relax their laws pro-

hibiting child labor. By 1943, 3 million kids, ages 12 to 17, were engaged in defense work.

cruisers (2 squares for each). Notice that the ships can be placed horizontally, vertically, or diagonally.

6. The goal of the game is to sink all of your opponent's ships. Use any method you wish to see who "attacks" first. Player One fires a "shot" by calling out a square—"B-7," for example. Player Two checks his or her Defense Grid. If no part of a ship is on B-7, Player 2 says, "It's a miss!" or "That shot missed!" If the shot hits one of Player Two's ships, he or she then says, "It's a hit!" and marks an X on that square on the Defense Grid. Player One marks his or her Attack Grid for every shot fired, with a dot for a miss and an X for a hit, as shown.

7. Player One calls out 9 more shots the same way—a total of 10 shots. A ship is sunk only when all of its squares have been hit. A player who scores a hit, therefore, should concentrate the next shots in the same area until the ship is sunk. When a player's ship is sunk, the player announces, "It's a hit and one of my cruisers has been sunk!"

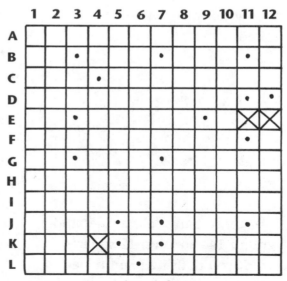

Attack Grid

8. After Player One has fired 10 shots, it's Player Two's turn to attack with 10 shots.

9. Players continue taking turns. But, once a player has lost a ship, he or she fires two fewer shots in the next round for each ship lost. If a player has lost three ships, for example, his or her next attack will consist of only 4 shots.

10. The battle is over when one player has sunk all of his or her opponent's ships.

PAPER AIRPLANE

Throughout the war years, America's skies were constantly crowded with the nation's warplanes— some on training flights, others on their way from factories to battle zones. It was natural for many young people to become experts in identifying the different models. Since the propeller planes of the 1940s flew lower and slower than today's modern jets, it was not hard to spot each plane's identifying features. Many kids even bought the handbooks used by the aircraft spotters and learned to identify the airplanes of other countries, including Germany and Japan.

Young people also constructed all sorts of model aircraft. They carved some from balsa wood and painted them in careful detail. They made others out of thin paper stretched across wooden struts, and still others of plain paper folded in different ways. The plain paper airplanes, like the one you'll make, were not as ambitious as the other models, but some of them glided beautifully and were great for distance contests. Try making several with a friend and see who can produce the craft that flies the farthest.

MATERIALS
1 sheet of paper for each airplane, 8½ by 11 inches
1 standard paper clip

1. Fold the paper in half the long way. Press the crease firmly, then turn the paper over and open it so the pointed edge of the crease is facing up.

2. Place the sheet flat on your work surface so that the crease is vertical. Fold the upper right-hand corner, marked *a*, down until it touches the center crease, as shown in the drawing. Press the crease firmly. Do the same with the upper left-hand corner, marked *b*.

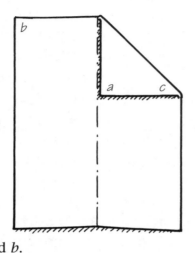

3. Fold point *c* over until it touches the center crease exactly at point *a*. Press the crease the whole length of the paper, as shown. Repeat with point *d*, folding it to point *b* and pressing the crease.

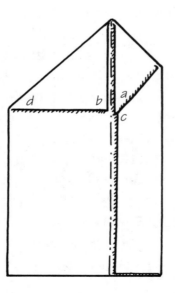

4. Pick up the paper by the center crease. Raise the wings a little by lifting up on points *c* and *d*.

5. Place a paper clip over the nose of your plane, as shown, and it's ready to fly. To fly the airplane, hold it by the center crease just about where points *a* and *b* touch the crease. Throw it with a firm, steady motion; don't throw too hard or the plane is likely to nose-dive. Experiment with your throwing motion, and also with the way you position the paper clip, and gradually your airplane will soar farther and higher.

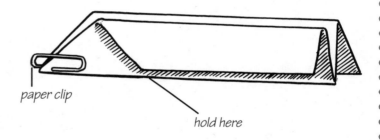

paper clip

hold here

PROJECT   JET-POWERED FLIGHT TEST

Throughout World War II, both Allied and Axis scientists worked constantly to develop faster aircraft. They steadily increased the speed and range of conventional propeller aircraft and they also experimented with jet-powered flight. A jet airplane achieves power by thrusting a jet of energy out the tail, and this thrust pushes the craft in the opposite direction, or forward. Modern rockets and spacecraft achieve lift-off in much the same way.

German aircraft specialists developed the world's first jet plane in 1939. Americans made their first jet test flight in mid-1942. Although a few jet aircraft were in use by 1945, nearly all of the planes flown during the war were propeller-driven. In this activity, you can demonstrate how jet propulsion works by creating a forward push from a jet of energy sent in the opposite direction.

MATERIALS

scrap of cardboard or poster board, about 1 by 5 inches
ruler
pencil
scissors
red and blue crayons or marking pens
drinking straw
transparent tape
15 to 20 feet of strong thread or fishing line
balloon (the long balloons work best)
helper (optional)

1. To make "wings" for your experimental jet craft, round the tips of the piece of cardboard or poster board, as shown, and cut a small V in the center to make taping easier.

2. Using crayons or marking pens, decorate the wings with the circled-star emblem of the U.S. Army Air Corps. The center of the emblem is red, the star is white, and the rest of the circle is blue.

3. Tape the wings to the straw, about 2 inches from one end. Use narrow (¼-inch) strips of tape to make as firm a hold as possible.

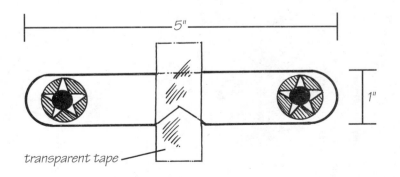

transparent tape

Women in Uniform

At the start of World War II, many Americans still believed that a woman's place was in the home, not in the factory or office, and certainly not in military service. By the war's end in 1945, that attitude had changed because 200,000 women had served their country well as WACs (army), WAVES (navy), women marines, and SPARs (coast guard).

There were even a few female pilots in the WAFS (Women's Auxiliary Ferrying Squadron), a unit of the army air force. The 2,000 WAFS helped the army overcome a shortage of pilots by transporting new aircraft to bases in the United States and overseas. Some of the women also flew test missions. The WAFS were never sent to the front lines, although twenty-eight of them were killed in the line of duty.

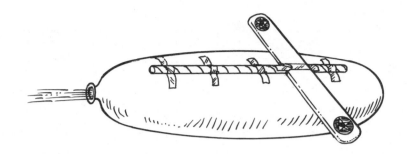

4. Run the thread or fishing line through the straw. Tie one end of the line to the back of a chair, or some other item of furniture, and the other end to another chair, stretching the line as taut as possible.

5. Have 2 or 3 pieces of tape ready, each about 1½ inches long, or have a helper ready to apply tape. Blow up the balloon. Hold the neck of the balloon closed with one hand and tape it to the straw with the other, or have your helper apply the tape.

6. As soon as the tape has been applied, let go of the balloon and watch the jet of air propel your experimental craft across the room.

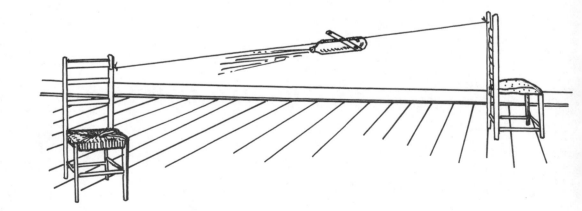

PROJECT PERISCOPE

Toy periscopes, first developed around 1900, became very popular during World War II, probably because of the importance of submarine warfare. Young people had fun using periscopes to try to see over crowds at events like parades and ball games. When toy companies switched to producing war materials, kids learned to make their own periscopes. They taped cardboard into a tube shape and set two mirrors at 45-degree angles. It didn't matter that these homemade periscopes were not very durable, because most of the fun was in the construction.

For your periscope, you can use a cardboard mailing tube instead of making a tube. Mailing tubes are inexpensive and can be purchased at many post offices and discount department stores. You'll need a tube that has a circumference (the distance around) of 8 inches or a little more. Measure the circumference by wrapping a tape measure or a piece of string around the tube. You'll also need two small pocket mirrors. These are available in the cosmetic sections of drugstores or discount department stores.

MATERIALS

cardboard mailing tube, with lids if possible: 8 inches
   around and 18 to 24 inches long
ruler
pencil
scissors
craft knife, to be used by adult helper
2 strips of cardboard, each 2½ by 7¾ inches
2 small mirrors, about 2 by 3 inches
white glue
transparent tape
adult helper

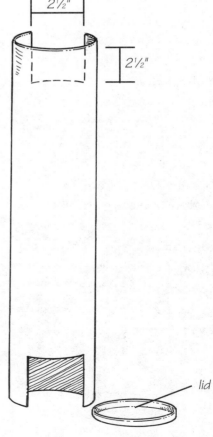

1. Remove the lids from the cardboard tube and set them aside. With the ruler and pencil, measure and mark an opening, or doorway, in one end of the tube, about 2½ inches high and 2½ to 3 inches wide.

2. Try cutting out the doorway with scissors. The cardboard is likely to be too thick, so ask your adult helper to cut out the opening with a craft knife.

America's "Silent Service"

More than 16,000 courageous sailors volunteered for duty in the U.S. Navy's "Silent Service"—the submarines of the nation's Atlantic and Pacific Fleets. Each of the 200 submarines operating in the Pacific carried a crew of eighty men who were forced to live in cramped quarters for six weeks or more on each voyage. When the war began, the crews were inexperienced and much of the equipment turned out to be faulty, especially the torpedoes.

As the men gained experience and the equipment was improved, the Silent Service began to play a vital role in the Pacific. Of the enemy warships sunk by the Pacific Fleet, almost one-third were victims of American subs. The Silent Service was equally effective against Japanese cargo ships, sinking more than 1,200. In addition, the submarines were used to report enemy fleet movements and to rescue airmen whose planes had gone down at sea.

3. Measure, mark, and cut a second opening on the other end of the tube, but facing in exactly the opposite direction, as shown in the drawing.

4. Place one of the cardboard strips on your work surface. Use the ruler and pencil to divide the strip into 3 sections, measuring 2¼ inches, 2¼ inches, and 3¼ inches.

5. Fold the cardboard on the lines you've drawn to form a triangle. (Hint: To make as straight a fold as possible, try bending the cardboard over the edge of a ruler.)

6. Before sealing the cardboard triangle with tape, attach one of the mirrors to the long (3¼ inch) section with white glue or by wrapping tape across the top and bottom of the mirror and onto the back of the cardboard.

7. Repeat steps 4, 5, and 6 with the other cardboard strip and mirror.

8. Close the open end of the cardboard triangles with transparent tape, so that they have one 90-degree angle and two 45-degree angles. These precise angles are necessary for the periscope to work.

9. Fit one mirror triangle into the doorway you made in the base of the tube. Make sure the mirror is facing up the tube at an angle. Place the lid on the bottom of the tube and tape the mirror triangle to the lid and sides of the tube.

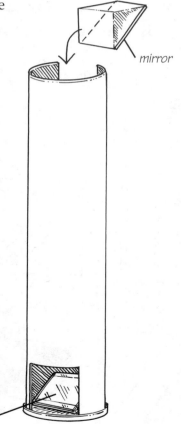

mirror

mirror

10. Fit the other mirror triangle into the doorway at the top of the tube, with the slanted mirror facing out. Fix it in place with tape. Your periscope is now ready to use to peer over crowds or to peek around corners!

If you have problems using your periscope, try adjusting the mirror angles.

AMERICANS ON THE MOVE

The Donatos were often amazed by how crowded their city and their neighborhood were becoming. All over the nation, people were moving from rural areas to the cities, eager for the high-paying jobs in defense plants and shipyards. Americans were on the move as never before, and one result was a tremendous housing shortage. Some of the Donatos' neighbors began renting out spare rooms, and several turned their garages into makeshift apartments. With encouragement from the government, some people transformed their homes into rooming houses, offering boarders a place to sleep and two meals a day.

Another result of this wartime migration was that Americans began to learn more about the people and customs of other regions of the country. Easterners, for example, like Frank's cousin Sophie, came to appreciate the

many Hispanic names and customs of California, and they enjoyed new kinds of foods, such as avocados and cioppino (che-PEEN-o), a fish stew. Sophie and her mom, in turn, introduced Frank's family to some Brooklyn favorites, including the hot dogs called "Coney Islands," and large soft pretzels served with mustard.

PROJECT CONEY ISLANDS

The hot dog—a frankfurter or sausage wrapped in a bread roll—was probably invented about 1900. A few years later, refreshment stands at the famous Coney Island amusement park in Brooklyn began selling a special version of the hot dog made by adding a thick meat-sauce topping. They called the new concoction a "Coney Island," or simply a "Coney." The movement of people during the war helped to spread the popularity of this all-American sandwich. Some street vendors today carry the recipe a step further by piling sauerkraut on top of the meat sauce.

INGREDIENTS

1 to 2 tablespoons butter or vegetable shortening
1 pound extra-lean ground beef
1 medium-size onion
2 tablespoons vinegar
2 tablespoons sugar
1 tablespoon dry mustard
2 tablespoons ketchup
1 tablespoon water
1 teaspoon steak sauce or Worcestershire sauce
½ teaspoon salt
tap water
6 frankfurters
6 hot dog rolls

EQUIPMENT

large skillet with cover
mixing spoon
cutting board (or onion chopper)
paring knife (to be used by adult helper)
medium saucepan
fork
kitchen tongs
small serving platter
adult helper

MAKES

4 to 6 servings

1. With an adult's help, melt a tablespoon of butter or shortening in the skillet. Crumble the ground beef into the pan and cook over medium heat, stirring frequently, with the mixing spoon. If the meat begins to stick to the skillet, lower the heat a little and add another tablespoon of butter or shortening.

2. Have the adult help you peel the onion and cut it into small pieces on the cutting board, or with an onion chopper. When the meat is nearly cooked (that is, with very little pink showing), add the chopped onion to the skillet. Lower the

Displaced Americans

One blot on the nation's proud war record was the way Americans of Japanese ancestry were treated. In the weeks following Pearl Harbor, the rage people felt about "the sneak attack" led many to believe that Japanese Americans might aid the enemy. The government ordered all Japanese Americans living on the West Coast to be moved to "relocation centers" in remote regions of the country.

During the spring and summer of 1942, 112,000 Japanese Americans, most of them born in the United States, were escorted by military guards to ten bleak camps, where they were forced to live for the duration of the war. All of those who suffered this treatment remained loyal to the United States. In fact, more than 8,000 of them were allowed to serve in the armed forces, and one Japanese American combat unit received more medals for heroism than any brigade in American history. In 1988, the U.S. Congress issued a formal apology to the 60,000 living survivors of the camps.

heat to simmer and cook the meat-onion mixture for about 5 minutes more. The onions should remain clear and firm, rather than soft and browned.

3. Stir in the vinegar, sugar, mustard, ketchup, water, steak sauce, and salt. Cover the skillet and simmer gently for about 15 minutes, stirring frequently. If the meat sauce begins to look watery, remove the lid and continue cooking.

4. Fill the saucepan about half full with water, and have your adult helper bring the water to a rapid boil. Puncture each frankfurter with a fork and use tongs to lower them into the boiling water. Turn off the heat immediately and let the frankfurters sit in the hot water for 5 minutes. (Frankfurterss are pre-cooked, so they only need to be heated before serving.)

5. Place the hot dog rolls on a serving platter. Drain the water from the frankfurters and place them on the rolls. Spoon the warm meat sauce on top of each Coney Island and serve.

PROJECT PHILADELPHIA SOFT PRETZELS

Since the 1890s, street vendors have been a common sight in American cities. In the 1940s, the vendors sold hot dogs, Coney Islands, popcorn, soft drinks, and other snacks from bright red and yellow pushcarts, usually with a glass box on top. In Philadelphia, some of the pushcarts featured a local specialty: large, soft, hot pretzels, topped with a splash of yellow mustard. As you'll discover in this activity, making soft pretzels requires some care, but the tasty results are worth the effort.

INGREDIENTS

1 cup very warm tap water
1 package dry yeast
1 tablespoon sugar
3 cups all-purpose flour
1 teaspoon salt
3 tablespoons softened butter or shortening
tap water
2 tablespoons baking soda
1 egg
3 to 4 tablespoons coarse salt (also called kosher salt)
yellow mustard

EQUIPMENT

small mixing bowl
large mixing bowl
mixing spoon
bread board, or clean countertop
wax paper
clean dish towel
table knife
rolling pin
medium-size saucepan, not aluminum or stainless steel
cookie sheet
spatula
paper towels
egg beater
pastry brush
adult helper

MAKES

8 large pretzels

1. Pour ¼ cup of very warm tap water into the small mixing bowl. (The water should be about 110 degrees F—warmer than lukewarm, but not so hot that it might kill the yeast.) Add the yeast and the sugar to the water and stir until the ingredients have dissolved. When the yeast mixture becomes foamy, you know the yeast is working.

2. Measure 2½ cups of flour and 1 teaspoon of salt into the large mixing bowl. Slowly stir in the yeast mixture, then the remaining ¾ cup of warm water. Mix thoroughly. The dough may feel a little dry at first, but that's okay.

3. Sprinkle a little of the remaining flour onto the bread board or counter top. Turn the dough onto it and let it rest for 5 minutes.

4. Wash and dry the two mixing bowls.

5. Rub a little flour on your hands and knead the dough for about 10 minutes: Fold the dough over on itself, then push it away from you with the heels of your hands. Now pull it toward you with your fingers, and fold it over again. Repeat these movements and occasionally turn the ball of dough over. If the dough becomes sticky, add a little flour. By the time you finish kneading, the dough should feel smooth.

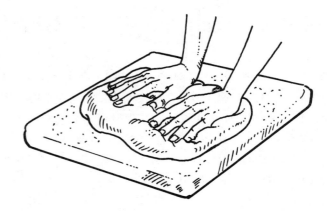

6. Use a small folded piece of wax paper to spread a thin layer of butter or shortening on the inside of the large mixing bowl. Form the dough into a ball and place it in the bowl. Cover the bowl with the clean dish towel and put it in a warm place for the dough to rise. (Yeast works best at a temperature of about 80 degrees.) Let the dough rise for an hour; it will just about double in size.

7. After an hour, remove the towel and punch down on the dough with your fist. This forces out some of the extra oxygen. Turn the dough onto the floured board or counter. Press it gently with your hands to flatten it into a rough square or rectangle shape.

8. Sprinkle a little flour on a table knife and cut the dough into 8 roughly equal pieces.

9. Sprinkle some flour on your hands and roll out each of the 8 pieces into a rope 20 to 24 inches long.

10. To shape a pretzel, pick up a rope by the ends and bend it into a U shape. Twist one end over the other, then press both ends into the base of the U underneath, as shown.

11. When all 8 pretzels have been shaped, let them rest, covered with a towel, for about 10 minutes.

12. Use this time to: (a) preheat the oven to 450 degrees F; (b) ask your adult helper to bring about a quart of water to a simmer in the medium-size saucepan; and (c) grease a cookie sheet with butter or shortening, using a small folded piece of wax paper.

13. When the saucepan of water is simmering, add the baking soda. Place a pretzel on the spatula and lower it into the water for about 20 seconds. Remove the pretzel, pat it dry with a paper towel, and place it on the cookie sheet. Repeat with the rest of the pretzels.

14. Use the egg beater to beat the egg in a small bowl for a minute or two. With the pastry brush, apply a thin coat of the egg to the top of each pretzel. (Remember to wash your hands after handling raw egg.)

15. Sprinkle the coarse salt over the pretzels and bake for 10 to 15 minutes. Check the oven frequently after 10 minutes. Have your adult helper remove the cookie sheet when the pretzels are golden brown. Serve warm with mustard.

RADIO SHOWTIME

Late in the summer, Frank's grandparents took him, Julie, and Sophie to a radio station to watch the broadcast of an afternoon soap opera. Although there was no action, it was exciting to watch the actors read their scripts into microphones, while a small group of musicians provided background music.

The kids were most fascinated by the sound-effects man. He sat behind a large table that was piled with the objects he used for making all sorts of sounds and noises. He produced thunder by shaking a large, floppy sheet of tin, clapped coconut shells on the table for the sound of a horse's hoofbeats, and crinkled cellophane in front of his microphone to create the crackle of fire.

As soon as they were back home, Frank and Sophie began writing their own radio script, with numerous ideas from Julie. They collected everything they could think of for producing sound effects, like rattling dried peas in a tin can for the sound of rain. On Saturday night, they delighted the family with their radio "broadcast." The following weekend, Frank's dad helped them put together a crystal radio so they could tune into broadcasts from their playroom in the attic.

PROJECT CRYSTAL RADIO

Radio broadcasting was barely twenty years old in 1942, but it had already become a major source of news and entertainment for millions of Americans. While very few young people had their own radios, many enjoyed constructing their own homemade receivers, called "crystal sets" or "crystal radios." Made from mail order kits or parts purchased at a radio repair shop, the sets enabled kids to tune in to their favorite broadcasts or explore the airways to see what distant stations they could hear. In many rural areas that did not yet have electricity, a crystal radio provided a valuable link to the rest of the world.

The few parts you'll need to purchase for your crystal radio are inexpensive and are available at many electronic stores, hardware departments, hobby shops, and radio/TV repair shops. Like kids in the 1940s, you'll experience a special thrill when you first hear voices or music from your homemade receiver.

Note: Like the homemade flashlight, your crystal set uses no household electrical current and presents no danger of electrical shock.

MATERIALS

about 40 feet of thin (22 gauge) insulated wire
scissors
wire cutter or penknife
hole punch
cardboard tube from bathroom tissue or paper towels
about 6 inches of electrician's tape or adhesive tape
small sheet of medium- or fine grit sandpaper
earphones with wire leads (no plug at the end)
germanium crystal (also called a "diode")
rubber band that fits snugly around the cardboard tube
adult helper

1. Place the wire on your work surface and use scissors or wire cutters to cut off a 5-foot piece. Ask an adult to help you use wire cutters or a penknife to strip about 1 inch of insulation off one end of the wire and about 3 inches off the other end. This will be your hookup, or connection, wire.

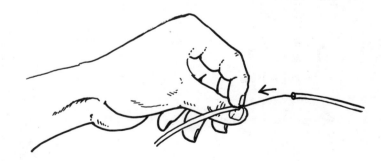

Wartime Radio

The war led to many changes in radio broadcasting. One of the first changes was a dramatic increase in news reporting, with many stations using more than 25 percent of their airtime for news, five times more than before the war. Another change was a ban on weather forecasting, so that the enemy would not be able to use the information to plan bombing raids. Programs that allowed listeners to request favorite songs were also suspended because enemy agents could use the requests, or the way they were worded, to send secret messages.

Radio broadcasting was also used for short messages to boost people's morale or the spirit of sacrifice. Some of these "spots" were catchy slogans, like "Pay your taxes; help beat the Axis." Other messages were simple reminders, such as "Every time you decide not to buy something, you help to win the war," or "Make your family a fighting unit on the home front!"

2. Cut a second piece of wire about 1 foot long. Strip about 1 inch of insulation off one end and about 6 inches off the other end. This will be your tuning wire. Set aside the tuning wire and hookup wire.

3. Use a hole punch to make 3 holes near one end of the cardboard tube, as shown by the letters *a*, *b*, *c* in the illustration. The holes should be about 1 inch apart.

4. Use the rest of the wire to make a tuning coil. First, strip about 1 inch of insulation from one end of the wire and push that end through hole *a* in the tube, as shown in the illustration. Now carefully wind the wire around the cardboard tube, one layer thick, with each coil touching the one before it, as shown.

5. When you've wrapped all but 3 or 4 inches of wire around the tube, punch a fourth hole in the cardboard *d* and push the last few inches of wire into that hole. Reach inside the tube and bend the wire back so it won't slip out. Cut a small piece of tape and use it to fix the end of the wire to the inside of the tube.

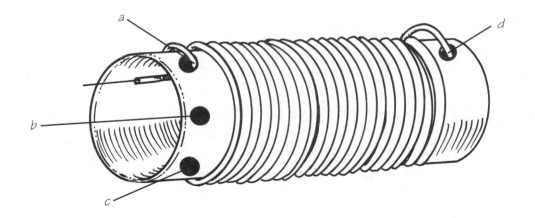

6. Use the sandpaper to rub the insulation off a narrow band of the tuning coil. This band should be about 1 inch wide (see illustration).

7. Separate the two wire leads of the earphone. The wires are very thin so work carefully to strip about 1 inch of insulation off each lead. Push one lead into hole *a*.

8. Next, push one end of the hookup wire into hole *a*. You'll now have three wires in that hole: the hookup wire; an earphone wire; and one end of the tuning coil wire. Twist the ends of these wires together, as shown, then wrap a piece of tape around the ends and push them out of the way so they won't touch wires coming through holes *b* or *c*.

9. The germanium crystal, or diode, has two wire leads. Bend these leads so that you can push one into hole *b* and the other into hole *c*.

10. Insert the second earphone wire into hole *b*. Twist this wire around the crystal wire that you put through hole *b* and wrap them with a piece of tape.

11. Pick up the tuning wire by the end that has 6 inches of insulation stripped off. Push this into hole *c* from the inside, so that about 5 inches of stripped wire stretches across the tuning coil, as shown.

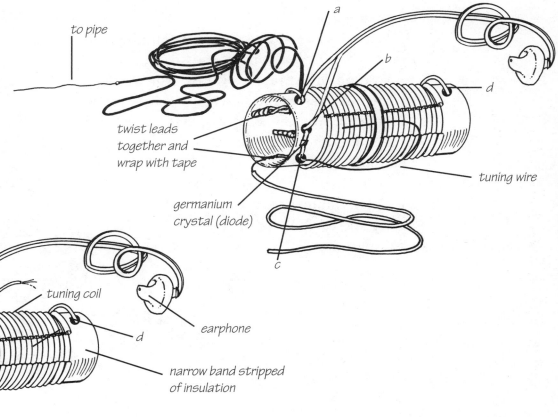

to pipe

a

b

d

twist leads together and wrap with tape

tuning wire

germanium crystal (diode)

c

hookup wire

tuning coil

a

b

c

d

earphone

narrow band stripped of insulation

12. Wind the crystal lead in hole *c* around a stripped part of the tuning wire inside the tube. Wrap the joined wires with a piece of tape. Well done! Your crystal radio is now ready to use.

13. Tuning Your Crystal Radio:

(a) With a piece of tape, attach the free end of your hookup wire to a cold water pipe, or the pipe on a radiator (but be sure the radiator isn't hot first!). This will connect your crystal set to a pipe system in your house that will serve as a huge antenna.

(b) Place the long, bared end of the tuning wire against the stripped band of the tuning coil.

(c) Position the earphone against your ear. Pick up the tuning wire and slowly move it across the tuning coil. (You can simply hold the other end of the tuning wire in your other hand and your body will act as an additional antenna.) When you hear broadcast sounds, move the tuning wire back and forth slowly and carefully until you have clear reception.

(d) To hold a station, slide a rubber band over the tube and use it to hold the tuning wire in place against the coil. Change stations by moving the tuning wire, then the rubber band.

(e) You can "turn off" your crystal radio simply by lifting the tuning wire off the tuning coil. But, since you're using free air waves, there is no special reason to disconnect it.

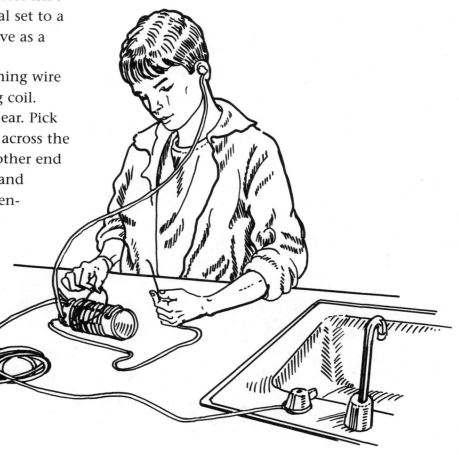

PROJECT SOUND EFFECTS

When radio audiences in the 1940s listened to a drama or a comedy, they weren't bothered by the lack of a picture. Instead, the combination of the actors' voices, the music, and the skills of the sound-effects director enabled listeners to create vivid mental pictures of the action. In this project, you can work with a friend to recreate those early days of radio, when people relied on their imagination to create the missing image.

You'll need a tape recorder with a microphone, a few household items to produce sounds, and a good deal of creativity. Work with a friend—or more than one—to think of a story, write the dialogue, and incorporate directions for the sound effects. A few sample sound effects are listed below to get you started. You'll find that experimenting is the best way to find what works, especially since recorded sounds are a little different from "live" sounds. For an added touch, try adding some background music, or even a few commercial breaks. When you're ready, you can either record the show all at once, as if it were a live broadcast, or record it in segments so you can re-record places that didn't work well.

MATERIALS

tape recorder with microphone
piece of stiff cellophane or wrapping paper
yardstick
electric mixer or blender
1 or 2 cups uncooked rice
shallow baking pan
pitcher of water
large bowl
2 paper cups
cardboard box filled with loose metal odds and ends,
    such as keys, tools, small toys

• For frying bacon (or eggs), crinkle cellophane softly. For a larger fire, crinkle the paper more vigorously and closer to the microphone.

• For gunshots, slap a yardstick firmly against a table top for each shot.

• For a motor running in the distance, run an electric mixer or blender at slow speed, 3 or 4 feet from the microphone. For higher speed, increase the power and move the mike closer.

• For a light rain, pour uncooked rice onto a shallow baking pan from a height of about 12 inches. For a harder rain, use more rice and increase the height. Add wind by blowing softly into the mike. By experimenting, you'll get the kind of wind sound you want and, with practice, you'll be able to create anything from a gentle breeze to a strong gale.

• For the sound of running water, like a stream, pour water from a pitcher into a bowl. Experiment with the placement of the microphone.

• For a person talking on the telephone, hold a paper cup close to your mouth and talk into the cup. Talking into a hat or a box also works.

• For a rider on horseback heading into the distance, turn two paper cups upside down and clap them on the table top. Have a helper slowly move the microphone away.

• For a crash, especially a comic crash like opening an overcrowded cupboard, rattle a box filled with loose metal junk, holding it close to the mike, then drop it to the table or floor.

CHAPTER THREE

AUTUMN

As Minnesota's summer heat gave way to cooler, shorter days, the Andersen family prepared for the autumn harvest. Earlier in the year, they had wondered how they would manage with Karl and the two farm hands in military service, but Shirley's parents had handled the spring plowing and planting alone, then hired high school students for the summer haying. Shirley did her part by taking care of most of the cooking and housework. With help from seven-year-old Edmund, she also took care of the two milk cows, the chickens, and the kitchen garden.

The school board also provided assistance at harvest time by allowing high school students time off to help bring in the crops. With this extra help, the Andersens—and many of their neighbors—produced a record wheat crop as their contribution to the war effort.

SPARE-TIME PROJECTS

Between school, homework, and household chores, Shirley didn't have much free time once school was back in session. She did try, however, to find a few minutes for herself almost every day, and she learned to treasure those moments. With a stew simmering on the stove for their supper, for example, she might take a little time to work on a pressed-flower bookmark for her friend Jodie's birthday, or to appliqué an apron for her mom. And, as she had often seen her mother do, she sometimes made colorful decorations for the house, including a vase of leaves preserved in glycerine water.

Even time was changed by the war when the government announced that the nation was going on "war time." This meant that daylight savings time—pushing clocks ahead one hour to provide more daylight—would not end in the autumn of 1942. Instead, clocks would remain ahead until the war ended.

Wartime shortages led many Americans to revive old crafts and hobbies. Since it was hard to find presents or household decorations in stores, people began making things by hand, as their grandparents and great-grandparents had done in the 1800s. Preserving leaves in a solution of glycerine and water was one of the many craft techniques that enjoyed renewed popularity in the 1940s.

For your glycerine leaves, you can use leaves that are still green or those that are just turning their autumn colors. Oak and maple leaves preserve well, as do ferns and even a few late flowers, especially those with clusters of blossoms, like hydrangeas. It's best to cut small, live branches because branches found lying on the ground might be dried out. The branches should be 10 to 14 inches long and slender enough to cut with scissors. Look for branches that have four to eight leaves; handle the branches with some care so that the leaves don't break off. Remember to ask permission from the property owner before clipping trees. Keep in mind also that you can't pick growing things in most state and national parks.

MATERIALS

scissors
3 or 4 branches with leaves
several sheets of newspaper
hammer
large, widemouthed bottle or jar (quart size or larger)
about 12 ounces glycerine (available at drugstores)
hot tap water
paper towels
tall vase

1. Spread several sheets of newspaper on your work surface and place the branches on top. With scissors, cut away some of the bark from the lower end of the branches, then use the hammer to mash these ends lightly, spreading out the woody fibers. This will help the branches absorb the glycerine solution.

2. Pour about 2 inches of glycerine into the bottle or jar. Add about 4 inches of hot tap water.

3. Place the broken ends of your branches in the solution and store the jar in a cool dark place, such as a pantry or closet.

4. After 3 or 4 days, start checking the leaves every day. If the glycerine solution is nearly gone, add more—1 part glycerine to 2 parts water. You'll probably notice that the color of the leaves is beginning to change; this is to be expected and usually results in some interesting hues.

5. After two weeks, remove the branches and dry the stems with paper towels. The leaves may feel a little oily and may even have tiny drops of oil on them. Wipe the leaves gently with a paper towel and arrange the branches in a vase. Your glycerine leaves will remain an attractive display for many months.

PROJECT **PRESSED-FLOWER BOOKMARK**

Many people use a plant press made of plywood, but for this project you can use five or six thick books. The blossoms you work with should be as fresh and free of moisture as possible. For this reason, it's best to pick flowers on a dry day, late in the morning after the dew has evaporated. Wild flowers such as daisies, black-eyed susans, and Deptford pinks will work well, as will garden flowers with flat petals, such as pansies and violets. Avoid plants with thick blossoms, like roses or day lilies. Remember to ask permission and avoid taking any plant material from public parks.

After you've made your bookmark, try using pressed flowers for other projects, such as notecards or a collage to put in a picture frame.

MATERIALS
scissors
6 to 8 blossoms, some with stems and leaves
paper bag or basket for carrying cuttings
several sheets of newspaper
paper towels
2 sheets of white paper
5 or 6 large, thick books
white poster board, 2½ by 7 inches

black ballpoint pen
white glue
small dish or plastic lid
tap water
craft stick or other stick for stirring
paintbrush, 1 inch wide
clear kitchen plastic wrap (optional)
hole punch
about 6 inches of narrow ribbon, any color

1. Cut the flowers with a few inches of stem and some leaves. Make clean cuts with your scissors, so that the stem isn't shredded. A collection of 6 to 8 flowers will give you plenty to choose from. Place your cuttings in the bag or basket and take them home.

2. At home, spread several sheets of newspaper over your work surface and place the flowers on top. Handle the flowers gently and as little as possible.

3. Place a paper towel on a sheet of white paper. Spread the blossoms on the paper towel, one layer thick. Put a second paper towel and then another sheet of white paper on top of the flowers. Place this paper-and-blossom "sandwich" on a large book and then stack 4 or 5 books on top.

4. Keep the flowers in this book press for 10 days to 2 weeks. Carefully check the flowers every 3 or 4 days. If the paper towels feel moist, replace them to speed the drying.

5. When the blossoms are dry, place more newspaper on your work surface and gently place your pressed flowers on top. The dried blossoms will be quite fragile, so use extra care in handling them.

6. Place the piece of poster board on your work surface and try to picture which blossoms might look good on it. If you want to include a name or a message, like "Happy Birthday," write it now with the ball point pen, leaving plenty of room for your pressed flowers. Leave enough space to punch a hole near the top of the bookmark.

7. Arrange 2 or 3 pressed flowers on the poster board. Use a spot of glue to attach each piece to the bookmark. Let the glue dry for 10 to 15 minutes.

8. Pour a little white glue into a dish and stir in a little tap water with the stick to thin the glue for easier spreading.

Wartime Farming

America's farm families faced an enormous challenge during the war. They had to provide enough food not only for the millions of people in cities and suburbs, but also for the 15 million men and women in the armed forces, as well as aid for the nation's allies in the world's war zones. In addition, the army and navy departments needed huge amounts of nonfood products, especially cotton and wool, for essentials like uniforms, tents, blankets, and bedding. To add to the challenge, farms were operating shorthanded because more than 800,000 workers left the farms for military service or for higher-paying factory jobs.

Through hard work and careful planning, the nation's farm owners achieved new production records each year. Although some food items were rationed to make sure there was plenty for the armed forces, the American people had more food than ever before in the country's history.

9. Gently brush a thin coat of the glue over the entire front surface of the bookmark. The glue will be white when you apply it, but it will clear as it dries.

10. While the glue will hold the pressed material in place, you can add more protection with plastic wrap—but you'll have to work quickly while the glue is still wet. Cut a piece of plastic wrap large enough to cover the front of the bookmark with a little overlap. Carefully place the plastic wrap on the bookmark and gently press it flat. Work any air bubbles out the sides with your fingers. Don't trim the part that overlaps the edges until the glue has dried completely (that is, has become clear).

11. Let the bookmark dry overnight, then use scissors to trim the overlapping edges of plastic wrap.

12. Use a hole punch to make a hole near the top or the bottom of the bookmark. Thread a piece of ribbon through the hole and tie it. Your pressed-flower bookmark is now ready to use or to give as a special gift.

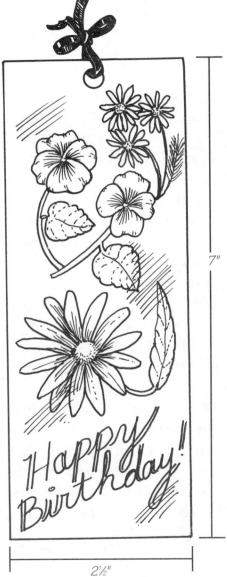

PROJECT · APPLIQUÉ APRON

Appliqué is the art of sewing (or applying) fabric shapes to a fabric background. This method of decorating clothing and other items has been used for centuries; early examples of appliqué have been traced back nearly 4,000 years. Appliqué became popular during the war years for two reasons: first, it was a good way to make use of fabric scraps left over from other projects; second, many people had practice in sewing stripes and insignias on the uniforms of family members in the military who were home on leave.

In this project, you'll use scraps of felt for your appliqués and apply them with fabric glue, rather than sewing them on. You can buy an inexpensive apron at a discount department store, or you can use the same technique to decorate a cloth book bag or backpack. Copy some or all of the appliqués shown here, or draw your own.

MATERIALS

several sheets of newspaper
apron, bag, or backpack, white or any solid color
2 or 3 sheets of white paper
pencil
scissors
fabric pen
scraps of felt, any colors (inexpensive remnants are available wherever fabrics are sold)
straight pins
fabric glue (available in sewing or craft sections of discount department stores)
permanent marking pen

1. Spread the newspaper over your work surface, with the apron or other item on top.

2. Begin by deciding on a plan for the project. Decide, for example, whether you'll use the farm-scene patterns shown here or create your own. Think also about how many appliqués you want, how large each should be, where you'll place them, and what kind of color combination you want.

3. Copy, or photocopy, the patterns on this page, enlarging them as needed, or draw your own creations on white paper. Cut out the patterns.

4. Place a scrap of felt on your work surface and position one of the appliqué patterns on it. Use the fabric pen to outline the pattern on the felt. Cut out the shape with scissors.

5. Repeat step 4 for the rest of your appliqué patterns.

6. Arrange your appliqués on the apron. Pin them in place so that you can move them around to create an arrangement you like.

7. When you're satisfied with the overall design, remove the pins from one appliqué, spread a thin coat of fabric glue on the back, and press it onto the apron.

8. Repeat step 7 with the rest of the appliqués.

9. Use a marking pen to add details, such as eyes on the farm animals. Your appliqué apron is now ready to use or give as a gift.

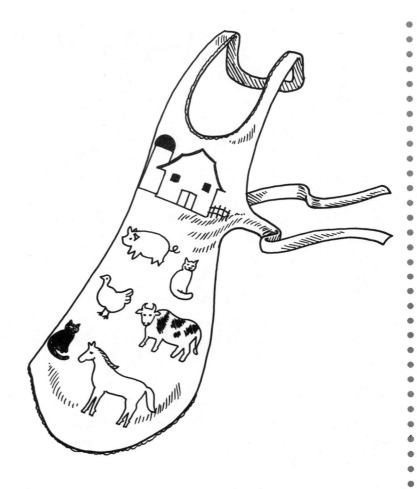

SHORTAGES AND RATIONING

In May, when Americans received their first ration books, Shirley asked to be in charge of the Andersens' books. She thought it would be a good way for her to contribute to the war effort. Since everyone received the same number of stamps in their books, no one could buy more than their share of scarce items like sugar and gasoline.

By autumn, however, the system had become so complicated that Shirley needed her mom's help to sort it out. Dozens of things were now rationed, and food items alone required two books for each person in the family—red for things like meat and butter, and blue for prepared foods, including canned goods. Adding to the confusion was the fact that the number of stamps needed for any item was likely to change from week to week.

With her mom's help, Shirley managed to make out a grocery list each week, counting out the right

number of stamps for each item. Her mom also helped her find substitutes for things that weren't available. Working together, they made substitutes like mock maple syrup and mock whipping cream. And, when the government urged people to observe "meatless Tuesdays" every week, Shirley found magazine recipes for meatless meals, like one for fondue that quickly became a family favorite.

 **FONDUE**

Many families first tried fondue during the war in their search for meals that were nourishing, easy to prepare, and used little or no meat. There were several different recipes, but the one that remained popular long after the war was called Swiss fondue (because it was made with Swiss cheese). Swiss fondue turned out to be a great dish to serve guests. A chafing dish or casserole in the center of the table keeps the fondue warm, and the diners dip chunks of crusty bread into it, twirling their forks to wind the stringy cheese onto the bread. For your first fondue, you can try either the Swiss variety or a firmer, less messy fondue using Cheddar cheese.

INGREDIENTS

½ pound Swiss or Cheddar cheese
1 cup milk
¼ teaspoon salt
¼ teaspoon dry mustard
1½ tablespoons butter
1 egg
French bread (baguette)

EQUIPMENT

paring knife
1-quart saucepan
cooking fork
small bowl
egg beater
mixing spoon
piece of wax paper
1-quart casserole
adult helper

MAKES
4 servings

1. Preheat the oven to 350 degrees F.

2. Ask your adult helper to help you use the paring knife to cut the cheese into small pieces.

3. Combine the cheese, milk, salt, mustard, and 1 tablespoon of butter in the saucepan.

4. Have your adult helper cook the mixture over low heat until the cheese melts, stirring frequently with the fork.

5. Break the egg into the small bowl and beat it lightly with the egg beater. (Remember to wash your hands after handling the raw egg.)

6. Add the egg to the cheese mixture and use the mixing spoon to blend the ingredients.

7. Use a piece of wax paper to spread the remaining butter on the sides and bottom of the casserole.

8. Pour the fondue into the casserole and bake at 350 degrees for 15 minutes if using Swiss cheese, 25 minutes if using Cheddar.

9. Serve hot. Break the French bread into bite-size chunks. Each person uses a fork to dip a piece of bread into the fondue, twirling the fork to break off the stringy cheese.

Shortages and the Black Market

Although the rationing system worked well, there were bound to be shortages. Coffee was in short supply, for example, because the cargo ships that transported coffee to the United States were needed for shipping war materials. As a result, ration coupons allowed coffee drinkers only one pound of coffee every five weeks—not even a cup a day.

One way to get around the rationing and the regulations was to buy on the "black market." The black market wasn't a place; instead, it was a term used to describe all illegal purchases. A store owner, for instance, might set aside a steak or a pound of butter for a favorite customer. People often referred to such transactions as "buying from Mr. Black." Organized crime was also involved; some gangs hijacked trucks of rare goods like sugar, and others printed counterfeit ration stamps. But most Americans were opposed to black market buying because it was unpatriotic as well as illegal, so the rationing system remained successful.

PROJECT COOKING WITH SUBSTITUTES

At different times during the war, some goods disappeared from store shelves completely. It didn't matter whether or not the items were rationed. Neither silk nor nylon stockings, for example, were rationed, but they were impossible to find because both materials were needed for making parachutes. Butter was rationed, but sometimes could not be found because so much milk was used to make cheese—the easiest way to ship milk products overseas. The sudden shortages could make meal planning difficult, but people learned to be flexible and often invented substitutes for whatever was missing. Here are two examples of substitutes to try.

Mock Whipping Cream

This recipe makes a fluffy topping that has fewer calories and more protein than real whipped cream.

INGREDIENTS

1 cup water
1 cup powdered milk
1 tablespoon lemon juice
½ teaspoon vanilla
1 to 4 tablespoons confectioners' sugar

EQUIPMENT

medium-size mixing bowl
mixing spoon
egg beater or hand-held electric mixer

MAKES

1 pint whipped topping

1. Combine water, powdered milk, and lemon juice in the mixing bowl, blending the ingredients with the spoon.

2. Mix the ingredients with the egg beater or electric mixer. As the mixture thickens, add the vanilla and 1 tablespoon of the sugar.

3. Taste for sweetness. Add more sugar until you have the sweetness you want—two tablespoons are usually enough.

4. Continue mixing until the topping is fluffy and light. Serve at once as a topping for baked goods or fruit.

Mock Maple Syrup

Real maple syrup was sometimes in short supply because of transportation problems, a shortage of farm workers, or the scarcity of both tin and glass for packaging, since both glass and tin were vital for war materials. When true maple syrup wasn't available, many Americans used this recipe for mock maple syrup. You can serve it as a dessert topping or at breakfast on pancakes, waffles, or French toast.

INGREDIENTS

⅓ cup of water
1 cup brown sugar (light or dark)
1 teaspoon vanilla
dash of salt

EQUIPMENT

small saucepan
mixing spoon
adult helper

MAKES

4 to 5 servings

1. Combine all the ingredients in the saucepan.

2. Have an adult bring the mixture to a boil. Stir frequently. Continue boiling, with almost constant stirring for another minute or two, or until the sugar has dissolved completely. Serve warm or at room temperature.

"Junk Will Win the War"

The song titled "Junk Will Win the War" was one of the many wartime reminders of how important it was to save every scrap item that could be converted into war materials. Radio stations, newspapers, and magazines provided other reminders in the form of conversion statistics. American families learned, for example, that a pound of kitchen fat contained enough glycerine to make powder for fifty bullets or six cannon shells. Thirty thousand razor blades had enough steel for fifty machine guns; just thirty lipstick tubes provided enough brass to make twenty bullet cartridges; 2,300 pairs of nylon stockings would make a parachute. And, if every family used one less can each week, in a year enough steel and tin would be saved to make thirty-eight cargo ships or 5,000 tanks.

JUNK needed for War
Scrap Iron and Steel

KARL'S SECRET

Late in the autumn, Shirley's brother Karl came home on leave before heading overseas. The family proudly escorted him into town for shopping, church services, and meals at his favorite restaurants. One thing that surprised Shirley was that he couldn't talk about where he was going, or when, or even what kind of aircraft he would be flying.

Karl carefully explained to the family how important secrecy was in wartime. Enemy agents could be anywhere, he said, and if they heard where a unit was going, or when it was leaving, they could alert enemy submarines or aircraft. Hundreds of American ships had been lost, he told them, simply because someone talked carelessly. Karl explained that all military orders and other vital pieces of information were relayed by secret code. If the enemy intercepted a radio message, or captured documents, they would have to be able to "break" the code before the information would make any sense.

Shirley and her friend Jodie became fascinated by codes, partly because both girls were trying to

keep secret diaries. Karl showed them how to make their own codes and how to decipher a code once they had the key. When Shirley asked him how he knew so much about codes, Karl just winked and said that was his secret.

PROJECT DECIPHERING SECRET CODES

People have been writing in codes, or ciphers, since ancient times. Some codes have been used to write secret letters or journals, and many have been created for military purposes. During World War II, the United States employed an estimated 50,000 code experts, called cryptanalysts, whose job was to try to decipher, or break, enemy codes and create new American codes. A major reason for the U.S. victory in the Battle of Midway was that cryptanalysts had broken Japan's code and could read every detail of the Japanese plan of attack.

In this activity, you can try your hand at deciphering two different kinds of codes.

MATERIALS
pencil
2 sheets of paper

Breaking a Caesar Cipher
One of the oldest—and easiest—codes to use (and to break) is called a Caesar cipher, used by Julius Caesar, the great leader of ancient Rome. To write in this code, both the sender and receiver use two alphabets. The first alphabet is the standard A to Z. The second is a shifting of the alphabet a key number of letters, using a secret key word.

1. In this example, the key word is PLUTO, so the second alphabet will be moved five spaces; the letters P-L-U-T-O appear at the start but are not repeated, so that the number of letters stays the same. Here are the two alphabets:

A B C D E F G H I J K L M N O P Q R S T U V W X Y Z
P L U T O A B C D E F G H I J K M N Q R S V W X Y Z

2. Using the Caesar cipher, with PLUTO as the key, a message saying "send help" would be encoded as: QOIT COGK

3. Here is a longer message, but with a new key word. Instead of PLUTO, the key will now be VICTORY. To break the code, write out the standard alphabet on a sheet of paper and, below it, the alphabet with the new key word. Here is the secret message:

PUJ PVHE TBSBNBJHN VP NJQPA KVNN PQMH IVCE

TWO TANK DIVISIONS AT SOUTH PASS TURN BACK

America's "Code Talkers"

In the war against Japan, the United States had a code that the Japanese could never break. A special unit of the U.S. Marines, made up of members of the Navaho nation, was assigned to every military unit. The Navaho "code talkers" used two-way radios to send and receive whatever military information was needed. Their secret code? The Navaho language. The Japanese had no trouble picking up the radio communications; but they could not decipher the messages because no one in Japan spoke Navaho. Throughout the war in the Pacific, the Navaho code talkers played a vital role in victory after victory.

Breaking a Checkerboard Code

In this system, which dates back to ancient Greece, a grid is made of the alphabet, and the rows and columns are numbered.

1. To read any letter, you would use the *row* first, then the *column*. The letter L, for example, is Row 3, Column 2, or 32. (Notice that Y and Z are in the same square; this is done to keep even rows and columns of five.) The word HERO would be encoded as 23-15-43-35.

2. Here is the Checkerboard Code for you to decipher. Write the coded message on a sheet of paper, then write the corresponding letter under each number.
11-45-45-11-13-31 11-45 14-11-53-34 53-24-32-32 44-15-34-14
11-24-43 41-35-53-15-43

ATTACK AT DAWN WILL SEND AIR POWER

columns

	1	**2**	**3**	**4**	**5**
1	A	B	C	D	E
2	F	G	H	I	J
3	K	L	M	N	O
4	P	Q	R	S	T
5	U	V	W	X	Y/z

rows

PROJECT COMMUNICATING IN SECRET CODE

Throughout history, people have created some very complicated systems in the effort to create a code that others could not break. One of the most elaborate was developed by Thomas Jefferson, third president of the United States. Jefferson's system required thirty-six separate wooden wheels on an iron rod; each wheel contained a scrambled alphabet around its edge. This system was actually used for a time in the early 1900s by the army, then by the navy.

Some other systems look just as complicated but are actually very simple, like the code you'll be using in this activity. Known as the "Fence" or "Pigpen" cipher, it was first developed in the 1500s and was later used by Confederate troops in the Civil War. German agents used it for a time during World War II because they could disguise the symbols in innocent-looking photographs, sketches, and even architect's drawings.

MATERIALS

2 pencils
2 sheets of paper
partner

1. With your partner, divide a sheet of paper into four shapes, as shown in the drawing: (1) a tic-tac-toe shape; (2) a large X; (3) a second tic-tac-toe; and (4) a second X.

2. Position dots, as shown, in the second tic-tac-toe pattern and in the second X.

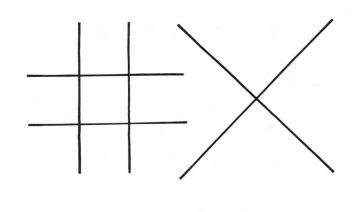

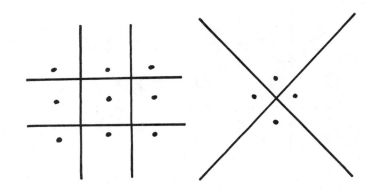

3. The four patterns contain twenty-six compartments. Arrange the alphabet in order, with a letter in each compartment. In the sample shown here, the letters are written from top to bottom—for example D in top compartment, F in bottom; J in top compartment, L in bottom. You and your partner can arrange the alphabet in a different pattern, as long as you are both using the same arrangement.

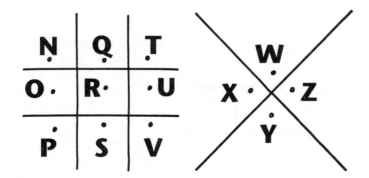

4. You can quickly see how easy this code is to use, especially if you've completed the previous activity. Someone who has never seen the code, however, would not know that a square shape is an E, or that a U shape with a dot is a Q. Practice writing a few letters.

5. For more practice, decipher the secret message. Imagine how hard it would be to recognize that those shapes were an important message, especially if they were disguised in something like a child's drawing.

∀ᒣ∧∧ ⅃ᒷᒷᒷ⅃⁊> ⅃ᒷ ᒫ Ǝᒷᒷᒷ
⁊Ǝᒣᑌ ᒪᒷᑌᒣᑌ⅃∀<ᒣᑌ⅃ᒣᒷᒷᒷ

MIDNIGHT
WILL ATTACK AT SOUTH COVE TUESDAY

CHAPTER FOUR

WINTER

The approach of winter gave the Andersen family time to relax and to look back on their first year of wartime farming. It had been a hard year, but they were pleased that their record harvest had made a contribution to the war effort.

The great majority of Americans, including the Andersens, seemed to be settling in for a long, difficult struggle to achieve victory. The fear and uncertainty that had gripped the nation in the early months of 1942 were gone, replaced by a firm confidence that the Allies would eventually win. The possibility of enemy air attacks also seemed less likely with each passing week. Almost every family, however, lived with the fear of receiving a government telegram reporting that a family member had been wounded or killed, or was "missing in action." That fear increased people's determination to do everything in their power to end the war as soon as possible.

"MAKE IT DO, OR DO WITHOUT"

The Andersens, like every other American family, had to deal with many different wartime shortages. Mr. Andersen liked his coffee, for example, but the ration system allowed the family so little that he sometimes tried to stretch the supply by brewing the used grounds a second time. Also, because Shirley and Edmund were growing fast, they used up all the coupons for shoes and boots.

One way to cope with the shortages was to live by the popular slogan:

Patch it up, wear it out,

Make it do, or do without.

Shirley and her friend Jodie made that slogan the theme of several slumber parties they had with three other girls. For part of the evening, while listening to records on Shirley's wind-up record player, they made use of old clothes and anything else that could be repainted, repaired, or re-used in some way. One Saturday, they painted and decorated old picture frames. They spent another evening sewing

colorful patches on jeans, turning the worn pants into the latest wartime fashion.

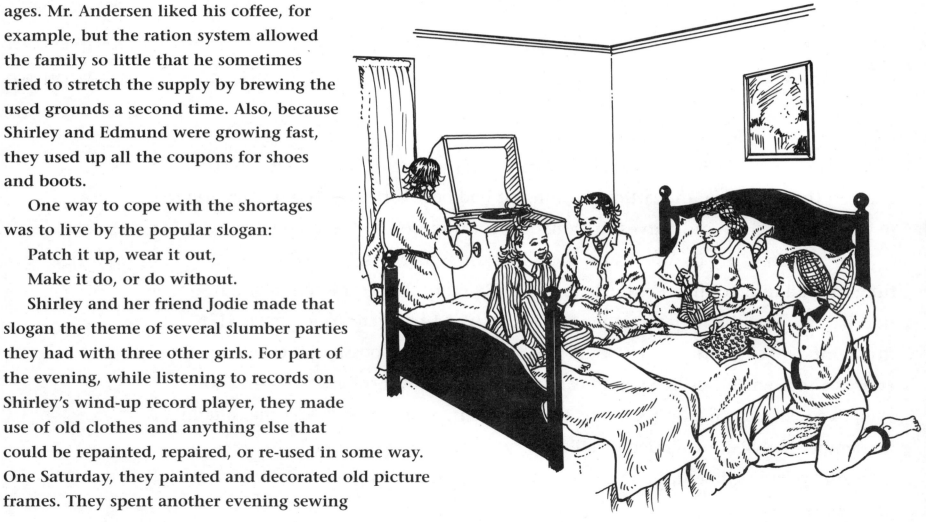

PROJECT PATCHED JEANS

The necessities of wartime led to many surprising changes, even in clothing fashions. For the first time in history, for example, it became socially acceptable for women to wear jeans or slacks in public, rather than skirts or dresses. The change was necessary for the safety and comfort of women working in factories and shipyards. While women welcomed the new trend, they had trouble finding women's pants in stores because of shortages and the increased demand.

One solution was to patch up old slacks and jeans. And, instead of looking for matching fabrics, many women began using brightly contrasting colors and some cut the patches in imaginative shapes. The patched jeans created a lively new fashion, one that has remained popular ever since. For your patching project, you can use an old shirt or a cloth book bag if you don't have a worn pair of jeans. For patches, you can buy fabric scraps, called remnants, in the fabric or sewing section of discount department stores.

MATERIALS

worn pair of jeans (or substitute)
scraps of fabric (most stores will sell you a bunch of remnants, giving you plenty to choose from)

2 or 3 sheets of white paper
pencil
ruler
scissors
fabric pen, or tailor's chalk (a pencil with soft lead will work, too)
6 to 8 straight pins
sewing needle
6-strand embroidery floss in colors to match, or contrast with, fabrics
black permanent marking pen

1. Spread out the jeans or other item you are going to patch and the fabric scraps on your work surface to plan your design. If you're not patching a particular worn spot, decide how many patches you want and where you want to place them. (Four or five patches are usually enough.)

2. Experiment with your fabric scraps, placing them in different spots on the jeans. Decide whether you want your patches to be simple squares

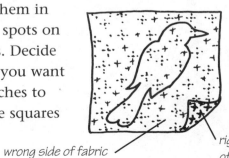

wrong side of fabric

right side of fabric

"Victory Suits"

In order to have as much cloth as possible for the needs of the armed forces, the government established guidelines for how much fabric should be used for each article of civilian clothing. One of the least successful recommendations was for a "victory suit" for men. The suit was made with no cuffs and no lapels, no flaps on the pockets, and very skimpy fabric throughout. Some men tried the suits out of a sense of patriotic duty, but they remained unpopular and the experiment was soon quietly dropped.

or rectangles, or other shapes like the sun and bird patterns shown on page 69. Make choices about colors, too, looking for attractive contrasts or complements, both in the patches and in the threads you use.

3. Draw the shape for each patch on a sheet of paper, using a ruler for any straight lines. Cut out all the patterns with scissors.

4. Place the pattern for one patch on the back (or wrong) side of the fabric scrap. Trace around it with fabric pen or tailor's chalk. Cut out the patch.

5. Repeat step 4 for your other patches.

6. Position a patch, right side up, on the spot you've chosen for it and pin it to the jeans with straight pins.

7. Decide what color embroidery floss you want to use, and cut a piece 18 to 20 inches long. The floss has six strands. Separate three strands and thread the needle with them, pulling the thread all the way through until only about 4 inches of floss are left. Tie a double knot near the end of the long part.

8. To sew the patch on the jeans, you'll use the whipstitch (also known as overcast stitch). To whipstitch: bring the needle up from inside the jeans, coming through both layers of fabric at *a*, as shown. Stitch over the edge of the patch, going down at *b*. Come up at *c*, go over the edge of the patch to *d*, and continue sewing all the way around.

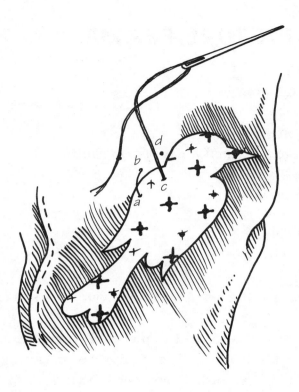

9. When you've stitched all the way around the patch, tie a double knot inside the jeans, close to your last stitch. Cut off the extra floss, and re-thread your needle for the next patch.

10. Use a marking pen to add details, like the bird's feet or eye, or the face on the sun.

11. Repeat steps 6–10 for additional patches. Your re-styled jeans are now ready to wear!

 **REFINISHED PICTURE FRAME**

Most repair businesses were closed "for the duration" (for the length of the war), so Americans taught themselves how to make simple household repairs. Newspapers and magazines helped with a steady stream of how-to articles. Many people also used their new skills to restore or refinish old items around the house, including tables, chairs, cabinets, and all sorts of smaller pieces.

For your refinishing project, ask an adult to help you find an old object to work on, such as a wooden picture frame, or an old stool, tray, or box. If you can't find anything at home, you can purchase an inexpensive unfinished item in the craft- or hobby section of a discount department store. The directions here are for a picture frame, but you can easily adapt them to any other object.

MATERIALS
several sheets of newspaper
wooden picture frame, about 10 by 16 inches, with
*   border 2 to 3 inches wide*
1 or 2 sheets of sandpaper, medium or fine grit
clean rag
1-inch wide paintbrush
1 small can or jar of latex or acrylic paint—white,
*   antique white, or light blue*

pencil
2 sheets of white paper
ruler
scissors
piece of thin cardboard or poster board, about 4
*   inches square*
clear mending tape
red acrylic paint
small dish
stencil brush

1. Spread the newspaper over your work surface.

2. Use the sandpaper to prepare the picture frame for painting. If the frame was previously painted or varnished, you need to sand it just enough to dull the finish—you don't have to sand down to the bare wood. Make sure there are no glossy or shiny spots. If this is an unfinished frame, a light sanding will be enough.

3. Wipe off the sanding dust with a clean rag and place a fresh sheet of newspaper on top of your work surface.

4. Use the paintbrush to paint the frame with a coat of white paint, antique white, or light blue. Allow the paint to dry according to the directions on the can or jar. Apply a second coat, if needed.

5. While the paint dries, draw the heart for your stencil on a sheet of white paper. The heart should be large enough to fit on the frame with a ¼-inch border above and below, as shown in the drawing.

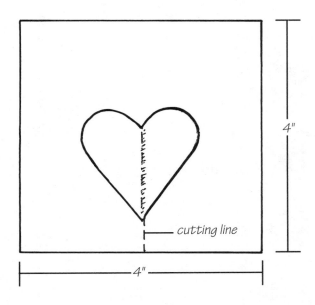

cutting line

4"

4"

6. Cut out the heart shape with scissors and place it on the 4-inch-square piece of cardboard or poster board. With the bottom of the heart about ¼ inch from the bottom of the cardboard, trace around it with pencil.

7. Use the scissors to cut from the edge of the cardboard to the bottom point of the heart, as shown, then cut all the way around the heart. Seal the cut at the bottom of the stencil with a piece of transparent tape.

8. Before you use your stencil to decorate the frame, practice on the second sheet of white paper. Pour a little red paint into a small dish. Holding the stencil brush straight up and down, dip it lightly into the paint. With the brush still upright, paint from the edge of the stencil toward the center. Go all the way around the heart in this manner, then fill in the middle. Lift the stencil straight up from the paper to keep from smudging the paint.

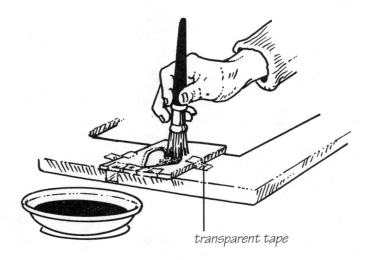

transparent tape

9. Plan to space the hearts evenly around the frame. Use ruler and pencil to make a mark where the left side of each heart should be.

10. Place the stencil on the first position you've marked on the frame. To hold it firmly in place, you may want to use 3 or 4 pieces of tape. Stencil the heart onto the frame, then carefully lift off the stencil. Let the paint around the edge of the stencil dry completely before you paint the next heart. Continue around the frame and your refinishing project is finished!

WARTIME CHRISTMAS

With Karl somewhere overseas in the army air corps, the Christmas season didn't feel quite right to Shirley and her family. The house felt empty without him, and they worried about how he was and even where he was, since he hadn't been able to tell them.

Then, two weeks before Christmas, they received a long letter from him. They learned that he was stationed somewhere in England and that he would be spending the holidays with an English family in a small village. The family's daughter, a nurse, had invited him and his best friend for the week. The family also had a son who was the same age as Edmund, and Karl promised to report what a boy's Christmas was like in wartime England.

Shirley felt better knowing that her brother was all right and she began to enjoy the Christmas preparations. Edmund helped her cut scraps of ribbon to make a banner to hang on the wall, and she showed him how to cut out paper snowflakes to decorate the tree and the windows of the house. In the kitchen, Shirley and her mother had fun with cooking and baking projects.

Along with the Christmas turkey and trimmings, they made an orange-cranberry sauce and a sweet potato pie.

PROJECT SWEET POTATO PIE

Holiday feasts during the war required a little extra planning because of shortages and the rationing of many food items, such as canned goods, sugar, and butter. While most kinds of meat were rationed, turkey and chicken were not. Potatoes weren't rationed either, so it was not unusual for families to serve two kinds of potatoes, such as mashed white potatoes and baked sweet potatoes or yams. In this activity, you'll try another delicious way to serve sweet potatoes—in a pie. After World War II, sweet potato pie declined in popularity for many years, but then experienced a vigorous renewal in the 1990s, especially in gourmet restaurants.

INGREDIENTS

2 to 2½ cups canned sweet potatoes
½ cup butter, softened (room temperature)
¾ cup sugar
2 eggs
1¼ cups milk
1 teaspoon vanilla
½ teaspoon salt
½ teaspoon cinnamon
¼ teaspoon ground nutmeg
¼ teaspoon ground allspice
9-inch unbaked pie crust

EQUIPMENT

fork
vegetable peeler
small mixing bowl
potato masher
medium-size mixing bowl
mixing spoon
egg beater
table knife
wire cooling rack
adult helper

MAKES

6 to 8 servings

1. Preheat the oven to 350 degrees F.

2. Place the sweet potatoes in a small mixing bowl. Use a potato masher or a fork to mash the potatoes.

3. Combine the butter and sugar in the larger mixing bowl. Stir them well with the mixing spoon, then use the egg beater to blend them.

4. Crack the eggs into the bowl. Mix thoroughly with the mixing spoon.

5. Add the mashed sweet potatoes to the mixture. Stir well.

6. Add the milk, vanilla, salt, cinnamon, nutmeg, and allspice. Stir the mixture well. If the mixture seems very soupy or liquidy, add another ½ cup of sweet potatoes, then pour it into the pie shell.

7. Bake the pie for 35 to 45 minutes. The pie is done when the filling is firm, or when a knife inserted in the center comes out clean. Have your adult helper remove the pie from the oven and place it on the wire rack to cool. Serve at room temperature.

Victory Mail

Letters to or from members of the armed forces were written on sheets of very thin paper called Victory Mail, or V-Mail. The paper was then folded up to make its own envelope. When people at home received a letter from someone in service, they were often disturbed to find that many words—or even entire sentences—had been blacked out. This was the work of government censors, men and women who read every piece of mail and cut, or censored, any bit of information that could possibly help the enemy. For example, if a soldier mentioned how many men were in his unit, or what kind of weapon he was training with, the censor would remove that information.

He's *Sure* to get
V···—MAIL
Safest Overseas Mail
U.S. ARMY POSTAL SERVICE

PROJECT HOLIDAY BANNER

Americans toned down their holiday decorations during the war years. Most families continued to have a Christmas tree with lights (although there were no replacement bulbs), but few decorated the outside of their homes with lights. People also made use of decorations from past years, or used scraps to make new items, such as wreaths, table centerpieces, and wall hangings. In this project, you'll use felt and scraps of ribbon or rickrack to make a beautiful wall hanging that will last for years. For Christians, the word Noel refers to the birth of Jesus; non-Christians sometimes use it to refer to a new beginning, such as peace following a war. If you'd like to use your wall hanging for Hanukkah, Kwanza, or some other holiday, you can use different letters or even cut out pictures for the panels.

MATERIALS

piece of red, green, or white felt, 8 by 42 inches
pencil
ruler
several sheets of newspaper
2¼-inch dowels, each 11 inches long
gold acrylic paint (optional)
small paintbrush (optional)
4 or 5 straight pins
sewing needle and thread in color to match felt

scissors
1 roll ¼- or ⅜-inch ribbon, 120 inches long—gold or other color to contrast with felt
fabric or craft glue
scraps of ribbon or rickrack, any widths, in variety of colors and patterns
16-inch piece of cord (gold, if available) for hanging banner
brad or small nail

1. Spread the felt on your work surface. Use a pencil and ruler to lay out your design on the felt. Follow the diagram on the next page closely, marking the five cross pieces to divide the banner into four 8-by-10-inch panels. Draw an outline for each of the letters to fit in the center of the panels.

2. Spread the newspaper over your work surface under the felt. Put the dowels on the newspaper. You'll be using one dowel as a hanging bar and the other to weight the bottom of the banner. The dowels can be left unpainted, or you may want to paint them gold to match the trim. Use gold paint and a small brush to paint about 2 inches on the ends of both dowels. Let the paint dry for 10 to 15 minutes.

3. Wrap the top of the felt over one dowel to enclose the dowel. Pin the fabric to itself on the back of the wall hanging, as shown in the drawing.

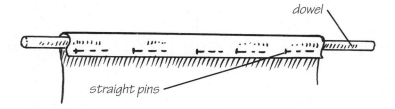

dowel

straight pins

4. Cut a piece of thread 18 to 20 inches long and thread the needle, pushing about 6 inches through the eye of the needle. Tie a double knot near the end of the longer piece of thread. Use a straight stitch to sew the fabric, making the casing just large enough for the dowel to slide in.

5. Repeat steps 3 and 4 for the dowel at the bottom of the banner.

6. Use the roll of gold ribbon to outline the four panels, as shown. You'll need eight 10-inch pieces of ribbon for the sides of the banner. (You may prefer to use two 40-inch pieces to make a solid border down each side, but be careful when gluing to keep the ribbon straight.) Measure and cut five pieces of ribbon to make the cross pieces.

7. For each section of ribbon, run a strip of glue along the felt, then press the ribbon onto the glue. Continue until you've outlined all the panels.

8. Cut scraps of ribbon or rickrack to make the letters in the same way. Use any combination of colors you wish, even mixing them on a letter. Spread glue along the line where the pieces will go, then press the ribbon onto the glue.

9. When all the letters are finished, tie the piece of gold cord to both ends of the top dowel. Use a brad or small nail to hang the banner, then step back and admire your addition to your family's holiday decorations!

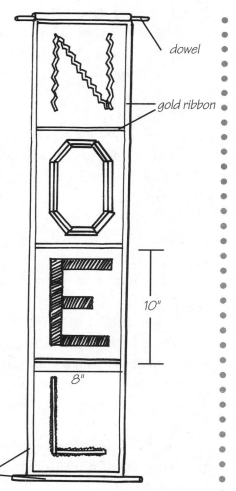

dowel

gold ribbon

10"

8"

gold ribbon

⬭PROJECT⬭ **PAPER SNOWFLAKES**

Paper snowflakes are fun to make because each one is different. After all the folding and cutting, it's always a surprise to unfold the paper and see what you've created. Since real snowflakes are six-sided crystals, most people make paper snowflakes that are also six-sided, as you'll be doing. The secret is folding the paper into the right cone shape.

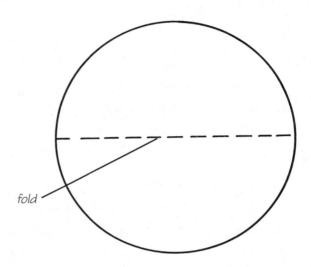

fold

MATERIALS

4 to 6 sheets of 8½-by-11-inch white paper
drawing compass, or any round object, such as a
    plate, 6 to 8 inches in diameter
old magazine
scissors
pencil
ruler
string, thread, or transparent tape

1. On a sheet of white paper, draw a large circle, 6 to 8 inches in diameter. If you use a drawing compass to make your circle, place an old magazine underneath the paper to protect your work surface. Cut out the circle with scissors.

2. With pencil and ruler, draw a line across the circle, dividing it in half, as shown. Fold the circle on this line.

3. Use the ruler and pencil to draw two folding lines on your half circle, dividing it in thirds, as shown in the picture. Fold the two side segments over the center one. Your folded paper will now form a triangle.

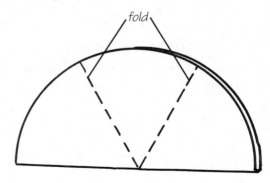

fold

4. Now fold the triangle in half, as shown, forming a cone shape.

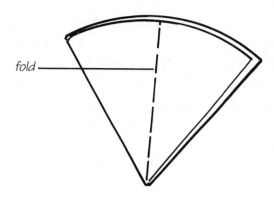

fold

5. With the scissors, cut into the cone shape, snipping out the paper. The dotted lines in the picture show many cuts in different shapes. Don't try to copy these cuts; the fun is inventing different ways of cutting into the cone to create different snowflake shapes. Unfold the paper and press it flat to see what you've created.

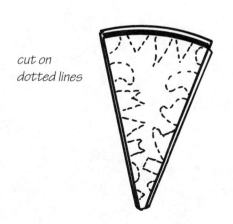

cut on dotted lines

6. Make more snowflakes, cutting the paper in different ways each time. Use transparent tape to hang some in windows and to decorate wrapped presents. Use string or thread to hang some from a Christmas tree, but make sure they don't touch any light bulbs.

A Colder Winter

Americans on the home front received a shock in the winter of 1942–1943 when they learned that there was a severe shortage of both oil and coal for heating homes. The shortage resulted from the enormous fuel needs of wartime industries, railroads, and shipping companies. In addition, American troops were now being sent to battle zones in Europe, North Africa, Asia, and the Pacific islands. This movement of men and materials required huge amounts of fuel for airplanes, tanks, trucks, and jeeps, as well as for cargo and troop ships.

The government devised a complicated system of fuel rationing. The goal was to assure that each family would receive two-thirds of the heating fuel they had used in the past. This would allow people to keep their thermostats at 65 degrees, about five degrees cooler than most people were used to. As with many shortages, this one reminded Americans that their sacrifices were small compared to the hardships faced by millions of people in the Allied countries.

 ## ORANGE-CRANBERRY SAUCE

Although canned cranberry sauce was hard to obtain during the war years because of the shortage of tin cans, the packaged berries were still available for traditional Thanksgiving and Christmas feasts. It was during the war years that many people began experimenting with new ways to use cranberries, apart from the traditional cranberry sauce. In this activity, you can try a tasty variation on tradition by adding orange to your cranberry sauce.

INGREDIENTS
1 12-ounce package of whole cranberries
2 medium juice oranges
⅛ cup water
¾ cup sugar

EQUIPMENT
colander
grater
small dish
paring knife
juice squeezer
3-to 4-quart saucepan
mixing spoon
fork
serving bowl
adult helper

MAKES
8 to 10 servings

1. Place the cranberries in the colander and rinse them under cool running water. Discard any berries that are blemished, unripe, or overripe. Set the cranberries aside to drain.

2. Ask your adult helper to help you use the grater to grate about two tablespoons of rind from the oranges into a small dish. Set the orange rind aside.

3. The adult can also help you cut the oranges in half with the paring knife. Use the juice squeezer to squeeze the juice into the saucepan.

4. Add the water and sugar to the orange juice.

5. Turn the heat on low and stir the ingredients steadily with the mixing spoon until the sugar has dissolved completely.

6. Add the cranberries, stir, and have the adult helper bring the mixture to a boil. Then, lower the heat and continue cooking at a gentle boil for 3 to 5 minutes, until the berry skins begin to pop. Turn off the heat and test the berries with a fork; they should be tender, but not mushy.

7. Have the adult remove the pan from the stove and pour the mixture into a serving bowl. Stir in the grated orange rind and let the sauce cool for about 15 minutes.

8. Chill the bowl in the refrigerator for about 2 hours. Serve cool.

HARDSHIP AND HOPE

A few days after Christmas, a powerful blizzard swept across the Great Plains, leaving behind a two-foot blanket of snow, with towering drifts that closed many roads. Electrical lines were down over a wide area, and the Andersens were without electricity for nearly a week. Their fireplaces provided enough heat and Shirley and her mom managed to use one of the old fireplaces for cooking and heating water, since the loss of electrical power also left them without a stove or running water. Mr. Andersen brought kerosene lanterns for evening light, but everyone in the family disliked the heavy kerosene odor, so they spent many evenings talking by the light of the fireplace.

As cold and dark as it was, the storm did inspire some new ideas for projects. The big rooster weather vane had been knocked off the barn roof, so Shirley's dad showed her how to make a little wind vane they could use to read the wind direction. Also, since the snow made it hard for the birds to find food, the whole family worked together to make suet cubes to hang from trees and the porch.

In the evening, huddled around the fireplace, the Andersens sometimes talked about how fortunate they were that the problems created by the storm didn't seem so bad compared to conditions in many Allied countries. Somehow, the storm made them feel closer to people in England and other war-damaged countries, because it gave them a tiny share in the hardships people were enduring.

PROJECT SUET CAKES

Many varieties of birds are fond of a little fat in their winter diet. By mixing suet, a solid fat from cows or sheep, with other bird food, you can provide them with both nourishment and a little internal warmth. Depending on where you live, your suet cakes are likely to attract chickadees, nuthatches, cardinals, grosbeaks, and many other species of birds. Hang each suet cake high enough off the ground so neighborhood cats and dogs can't reach it or its feathered visitors. When you see how much the birds like your suet cake, you'll want to have a fresh one ready all the time. Remember, however, to discard the cake when the weather turns warm, since spoiled suet will make birds ill.

MATERIALS

1 pound suet (available at supermarket meat
    departments)
cutting board
paring knife
heavy frying pan with cover
mixing spoon
1½ cups birdseed (mixed seed available at any
    supermarket or garden store)
½ cup other filler (leftover bits of bacon, cheese,
    cookies, dried fruit)

clean empty milk carton
paper towels
string or twine
adult helper

1. Place the suet on a cutting board and have an adult help you cut it into small chunks with the paring knife.

2. Put the cut-up suet in the frying pan, cover the pan, and heat it over medium heat. Hot suet tends to splatter, so use caution when you lift the lid to see if it has melted.

3. When all of the suet has melted, except for any crispy lean pieces, turn off the heat. Let the pan cool for 25 to 30 minutes.

4. Slowly stir in the birdseed and other filler. Don't stir too vigorously or you'll create a lot of crumbs. Let the mixture sit for another 10 minutes or so, until it feels lukewarm or cool but has not yet started to turn solid.

5. Spoon the mixture into the milk carton. Gently tap down the mixture with a spoon to release any pockets of air.

Holiday Travel

Nationwide gasoline rationing went into effect on December 1, 1942, and the American people discovered that travel was going to be difficult. Car owners were given stickers to display on their windshields. Most families received enough fuel for necessary travel but not for pleasure. For the next three years, automobile travel decreased 80 percent from what it had been before the war.

Many people turned to the railroads for long-distance travel, but the millions of men and women in the armed forces had travel priority. (Those priorities made air travel completely impossible for civilians.) Railroad stations and trains became so crowded that one railroad company's ad warned: "It is only fair to tell you that trains are crowded these days. You'll be more comfortable at home."

6. Use a paper towel to wipe any of the mixture that has spilled onto the side of the carton. Place the carton on another paper towel and refrigerate overnight.

7. By morning, your suet-seed mix will be quite solid. Cover your work surface with a paper towel and carefully peel away the cardboard carton. Leave the suet cake on the paper towel.

8. Tie string or twine around the cake in two directions, as if you were tying a package. Tie a knot at the top of the package, leaving at least 6 inches of the end of the string so you can hang your suet cake from something outdoors.

9. Tie the suet cake to a clothesline, porch railing, or tree branch. Make sure it's high enough off the ground so that four-footed animals can't reach it. Within a day or two, maybe sooner, the birds will discover your winter present.

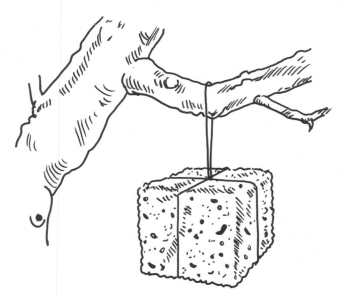

PROJECT WIND VANE

Wind direction can provide important clues about approaching weather. In most areas of the United States, for example, wind coming from the west or northwest usually brings fair weather; if there is rain, it is likely to be moderate. The most severe storms are likely to come with winds from the northeast, east, or southeast. Farm families have relied on wind vanes (also called weather vanes) for centuries to help them detect changes in wind direction. Modern weather forecasting stations continue to use wind direction as one of the key factors in weather prediction. In this activity, you'll make a simple but accurate wind vane that you can use to look for indications of a change in the weather.

MATERIALS

several sheets of newspaper
10-inch-square piece of heavy cardboard, or scrap
  of plywood
small empty yogurt container or sturdy 9-ounce
  paper cup
4-ounce piece of self-hardening clay or modeling clay
pencil
2 thin pieces of dowel, ¼ inch or less: 1 6-inch piece
  and 1 8-inch
ruler
sandpaper, medium or fine grit, or a wood file

scraps of construction paper or other heavy paper,
  any color
scissors
white glue
permanent marking pen, any color
directional compass (optional)

1. Spread the newspaper over your work surface; put the cardboard square, yogurt container, and clay on it.

2. Form the clay into a round, flat disk, about 1 inch thick, and place it in the middle of the cardboard. The disk should be a little larger than the top of the yogurt container or cup.

3. Press the yogurt container, upside down, into the clay, as shown in the drawings.

4. With the pencil, make a hole in the middle of the base of the yogurt container. Push the 6-inch dowel through the hole and straight down into the clay. Twirl the dowel around 3 or 4 times to make the hole in the clay large enough so that the dowel will be able to turn freely, but will be held perfectly upright by the clay. (If the clay base shrinks as the clay dries, use some white glue to fix the yogurt cup in place.)

5. Use a file or a piece of sandpaper to make a flat area or groove, about ¼ inch wide, exactly in the middle of the 8-inch dowel. (You'll be gluing the top of the 6-inch dowel to this flattened area.)

6. Use the ruler and pencil to mark a 3-inch square of construction paper. Cut out the square and fold it on the diagonal, as shown, forming a triangle.

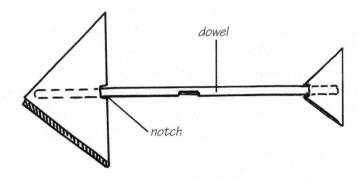

7. Now cut out a notch in the long side of the triangle, just large enough for the dowel to fit through. (See diagram.) Push the 8-inch dowel through the notch to the very tip of the triangle. Apply white glue to the dowel and to the inside of the triangle and press the sides of the triangle together. The dowel should now look like an arrow.

8. Make a stabilizer triangle for the other end of the dowel using a 1½-inch square of construction paper. This time, cut the notch at the point of the arrow, insert the dowel through the notch, and glue in place, as shown.

clay base

9. Glue the arrow dowel to the upright 6-inch dowel. Your wind vane is now ready to test.

10. Place your wind vane outdoors on a level surface, such as a picnic table. If you know which direction is north, write N on your cardboard base with the marking pen, and position the base so the N points north. (If you don't know the direction, ask someone who knows, or use a compass.) Add S for south opposite the N; E, for east, to the right of the north-south line and W to the left. Watch how your vane picks up the breeze and points in the direction the wind is blowing. See if you can use your wind vane to pick up changes in wind direction, then guess what those changes might tell you about the approaching weather.

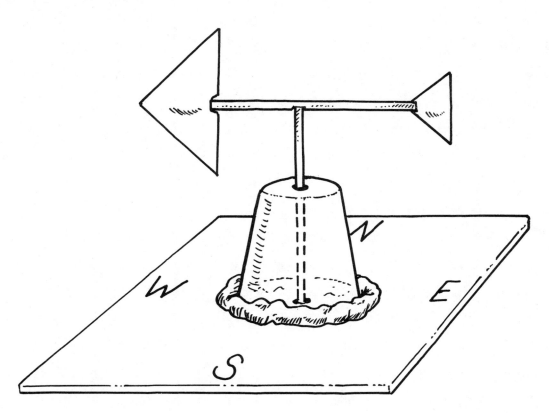

GLOSSARY

aircraft spotters   Volunteers who identified and reported every airplane that entered their area to guard against a surprise enemy air attack.

Allies   The nations that joined with the United States against the Axis powers during World War II.

alto   A Latin word meaning "high," used to describe cloud forms.

army air corps   The air force of the U.S. Army during World War II that was later separated from the army to become the U.S. Air Force.

appliqué   The craft of applying fabric shapes to a larger fabric.

Axis   The term used to describe Nazi Germany, militarist Japan, fascist Italy, and several smaller countries that followed Hitler's plan for world conquest.

Battle of Coral Sea   America's first naval victory over Japan, fought in May 1942.

Battle of Midway   This American naval victory in June 1942—a battle in which the opposing fleets were never in sight of each other—placed Japan on the defensive for the remainder of the war.

black market   The practice of illegally selling rationed items or counterfeit ration books.

blackouts   Air raid drills conducted at night, during which no lights were to be visible from businesses or homes that might serve as a guide to enemy bomber pilots in case of a real air raid.

Caesar cipher   One of the oldest secret codes. It used a key word at the start of a second alphabet.

Checkerboard code   An ancient code system using a grid of rows and columns.

cipher   A secret code.

cirrus   A Latin word used to describe wispy clouds.

civilian defense   Government officials and several million volunteers who organized wartime efforts on the home front during World War II.

"code talkers"   Navaho radiomen serving with American forces in the Pacific region, who used the Navaho language as a secret code because it could not be translated by the Japanese.

"Coney Islands"   Hot dogs topped with meat sauce, first developed by vendors at New York's Coney Island amusement park.

convoys   The naval system of combining twenty or more cargo ships with a fleet of warships that could provide protection against German submarine attacks.

cryptanalyst   A person who works with secret codes.

crystal radio or **crystal set**   A simple radio receiver made with a crystal diode, antenna wire, and earphones. It enables the listener to pick up radio stations without using electrical current.

cumulus   A Latin word for clouds that look like a "pile" or "heap."

dimouts   The dimming of signs and vehicle headlights along the Atlantic Coast, designed to stop German submarine commanders from spotting Allied ships in silhouette.

diode   (or germanium crystal) The crystal used to make a crystal radio.

Fence cipher   A secret code made up of Xs and tic-tac-toe patterns. It was developed in the 1500s, and used by Confederate soldiers during the Civil War.

germanium crystal   (or diode) The crystal used to make a crystal radio.

Ground Observation Corps   The official name of the volunteer airplane spotters who reported all aircraft that flew over their areas.

jet aircraft Airplanes developed in the early 1940s that used jet propulsion to push the aircraft, rather than the propeller system of pulling the plane; jet aircraft were not widely used during World War II.

Meatless Tuesday A voluntary program in which the government urged people not to eat meat on Tuesdays, which would make more meat available to ship to the armed forces.

"Mr. Black" A term often used to refer to the black market, or to an individual who dealt in black market goods.

mobile The artform of placing objects in balance so that they will move with air currents.

Morse Code The standard telegraph code of dots and dashes developed in the mid-1800s by Samuel F. B. Morse and still used today.

Nazi Germany The European nation, led by Adolf Hitler, that was the major enemy of America and its Allies during World War II.

nimbus The Latin word used to describe "a dark rain cloud."

Pearl Harbor The American naval base at Honolulu, Hawaii, which was attacked by Japan on December 7, 1941.

Pigpen cipher   See Fence cipher.

rationing   The system of requiring coupons for the purchase of scarce items so that everyone had an equal share.

relocation centers   The camps where 110,000 Japanese Americans were forced to live during the war because of government fears that some might be spies or saboteurs. Years later, the government formally apologized for this injustice.

Silent Service   The nickname for the courageous men who served in America's submarine fleet.

sneak attack   The term used to describe Japan's surprise attack on Pearl Harbor.

stratus   The Latin word for clouds that are "layered" or "spread out."

SPAR   The women's auxiliary corps serving with the Coast Guard.

U-boats   A common name for German submarines.

V   A common wartime symbol that stood for "V for Victory."

Victory garden   The remarkably successful system in which Americans grew table vegetables wherever they could find a little space. In 1944, the peak year, this accounted for 40 percent of the vegetables consumed by Americans.

Victory Mail or **V-Mail**   Letters written on thin paper that folded to become an envelope, making them very lightweight.

Victory Suit   A man's suit without lapels or pocket flaps. An unsuccessful attempt by the government to conserve fabric.

WACs   Women's Army Corps, the largest of the auxiliary military units for women.

WAFS   Women's Auxiliary Ferrying Squadron. Women pilots attached to the army air corps helped make up for an early shortage of pilots by ferrying airplanes to military bases and to overseas posts.

WAVES   Women Accepted for Volunteer Emergency Service—the women's auxiliary force of the U.S. Navy.

BIBLIOGRAPHY

Ronald H. Bailey and Editors of Time-Life Books. *World War II: The Home Front, USA*. Alexandria, VA: Time-Life Books, 1977.

Suzanne I. Barchers and Patricia C. Marden. *Cooking Up U.S. History: Recipes and Research to Share with Children*. Chicago: Teachers Ideas Press, 1991.

George Barr. *Fun With Science*. New York: Dover Publications, 1993.

Better Homes & Gardens. *Treasury of Christmas Ideas*. New York: Meredith Press, 1966.

Steven Caney. *Kid's America*. New York: Workman Publishing Co., 1978.

Editors of Time-Life Books. *Recipes: American Cooking*. New York: Time-Life Books, 1968.

Gven Evrard. *Homespun Crafts from Scraps*. Piscataway, NJ: New Century, 1982.

Martin Gardner. *Codes, Ciphers, and Secret Writing*. New York: Dover Publications, 1972.

Jill Jarnow. *RE-Do It Yourself*. New York: The Dial Press, 1977.

Alison Jenkins. *Creative Country Crafts*. Philadelphia: Running Press, 1994.

Lee Kennett. *For the Duration: The U.S. Goes to War—Pearl Harbor–1942*. New York: Charles Scribner's Sons, 1985.

David C. King and others. *The United States and Its People*. Menlo Park, CA: Addison-Wesley Publishing Co., 1995.

Richard R. Lingeman. *Don't You Know There's A War On? The American Home Front, 1941–1945*. New York: G. P. Putnam's Sons, 1970.

Susan Milord. *Adventures in Art: Art and Craft Experiences for 7- to 14-Year-Olds*. Charlotte, VT: Williamson Publishing Co., 1990.

Gabriel Reuben. *Electricity Experiments for Children*. New York: Dover Publications, 1968.

Lawrence Dwight Smith. *Cryptography: The Science of Secret Writing*. New York: Dover Publications, 1971.

INDEX